LOST PROPHECIES OF THE FUTURE OF AMERICA

Michael Snyder

CONTENTS

CHAPTER 1 - CORONAVIRUS AND THE COMING PANDEMICS

This book is the most difficult project that my wife and I have ever untaken, but it is also the most important. Over the past 10 years, I have written thousands of articles, my websites have been viewed more than 100 million times, I have authored four other books and I have done interviews with radio programs, podcasts and television shows all over the globe. My wife and I have been sounding the alarm for a very long time, but this book represents the most important warning of them all. What you are about to read is the product of literally hundreds of hours of research, and the information contained in these pages is beyond alarming. As you go through this book, at some point most of you will come to the realization that what we are sharing with you is very real, and that should chill you to the core. We really are heading into the most chaotic period in all of human history, and the events that we are about to witness are going to be more horrible than most people would dare to imagine.

But I want to stress at the outset that the purpose of this book is not to scare you.

Most people are going to respond to the things that will be coming upon this planet with great fear, but the purpose of this book is to give you hope.

God knew about all of these things in advance, He is in control, and He has a plan.

And He has sent us specific warnings about all of the things that are coming so that we would not be afraid. Yes, all of our lives are about to change dramatically. But just because your future may look a lot different than you originally envisioned, that doesn't mean that it will be a bad future. We must be willing to embrace what God has planned, because He knows what we truly need more than we do. And if you are willing to accept the fact that God's plan is far superior to any plan that you could have ever come up with, that will help you to have peace during all of the chaos that is approaching.

For decades, people have been having supernatural experiences in which God has shown them what will happen if America does not turn away from evil. The supernatural experiences are often very detailed and they are remarkably consistent with one another. In this book you will read hundreds of direct quotes from various prophetic voices, and you will be amazed at how perfectly they all line up with one another, and that is because they all come from the same source.

I knew that I was supposed to write this book all the way back in 2016, but I also knew that the timing had to be right. Most people were not ready for this message in 2017, 2018 or 2019, and so even though I kept talking with my wife about this book throughout those years, I never moved forward with it.

But then in the second half of 2019 I began to feel a tremendous sense of urgency to get this book out, and during my prayer times the Lord kept putting the year 2020 on my heart. I kept sensing that 2020 was going to be a major turning point, and I shared that repeatedly with those that I know. I knew that I had to get this book out, because prophetic events were going to begin greatly accelerating.

Even though I can tend to be long-winded, I am going to try to keep this book short because I want people to be able to afford multiple copies so that they can give them to family and friends. We will not always be able to share this sort of information on the Internet, and so it is imperative for people to have hard copies of these prophecies in their hands. In fact, if you purchased a digital version of this book I very much encourage you to get a physical copy as well. God didn't specifically warn us about what is coming so that we would be afraid, but rather so that we would not be afraid. There is hope in understanding what is going to happen, and there is hope in getting prepared for it. And as these prophecies come to pass one after another, many will finally understand that the God of the Bible is very real, and this will result in multitudes being saved. So please get physical copies of this book, because this book will be an indispensable tool in the years ahead.

Unfortunately, most people have absolutely no idea what is ahead of us. As events increasingly spin out of control, many of those that do not understand what is happening will be overwhelmed by their emotions. Some will respond with tremendous anger and frustration, while others will give in to anxiety, depression and despair. Late last year, I wrote an article about how the suicide rate in the U.S. had soared to an all-time record high, and it will likely go much higher as our society gets hit by one major crisis after another.

But there is absolutely no reason why anyone should ever commit suicide. In fact, if you truly understand the bigger picture there is absolutely no reason to view the future negatively at all.

Personally, there is no other time in human history that I would have rather lived in than right now. I believe that this will be the greatest hour for the people of God, and I believe that the greatest chapters of my life are still ahead of me.

Yes, things are going to get really, really crazy. But it is when times are the darkest that heroes are needed the most. You were created for such a time as this, and God put you at this specific moment in history for a reason.

And those that know Jesus understand that any trials that we will face are just temporary. The end of the book says that we win in the end, and we have an eternal reward waiting for us that is so great that it makes any pain and suffering that we must suffer in this life relatively insignificant.

If you have your eyes on Jesus and the things that are eternal, you will be able to get through whatever is ahead.

But if your life is all about the things of this world, and you can't let go of your own plans and ambitions for this life, the events that are rapidly approaching will be exceedingly painful for you.

There is hope in understanding what is coming, there is hope in getting physically, mentally, emotionally and spiritually prepared for those events, and there is hope in trusting that God has everything in His hands no matter what happens.

Some of you will live through the disasters that I detail in this book and some of you won't. But if you know Jesus, we will all wind up at the same destination in the end.

If you do not know Jesus, I would very much encourage you to go straight to the final chapter of this book. Those that know Jesus will always have hope even during the darkest of days, but those that do not know Jesus will not have any hope during the nightmares that are coming.

For those of us that are believers, it should not come as a surprise that we are moving into deeply troubled times. The Scriptures tell us that the period of time just before the return of the Lord Jesus Christ will be the most chaotic time in human history, and Jesus gave us specific signs to watch for so that we would know when His return was getting close. In Luke 21:11, Jesus specifically identified "pestilences" as one of those signs...

11 And great earthquakes shall be in divers places, and famines, and pestilences; and fearful sights and great signs shall there be from heaven.

We do not know if COVID-19 is one of the "pestilences" that Jesus was referring to in that verse, but without a doubt "pestilences" are clearly one of the signs that Jesus told us to be watching for.

And in more recent times, God has given people supernatural experiences in which they were shown more specifics about what we should expect regarding these "pestilences" of the last days.

For example, while he was still alive a wonderful man of God named John Paul Jackson was shown that the world would soon enter a time of great chaos. He described this period of time as "the perfect storm", and he warned that it would be unlike anything we have ever faced before. During this "perfect storm", he was shown that we would have to deal with more than one pandemic...

The Lord told me there would be a pandemic that came, but the first one would prove to be little but fear. But the second one that comes would be serious. So there is a pandemic that is going to be coming.

Source: https://bit.ly/2BDArBr

The first portion of that prophecy appears to have been precisely fulfilled. The global coronavirus outbreak that we are witnessing right now has officially been designated as a "pandemic" by the World Health Organization, and it has killed hundreds of thousands of people. But it has become clear that it isn't going to kill more than 50 million people like the Spanish Flu pandemic of 1918 to 1920 did.

However, there is absolutely no debate that COVID-19 has caused a tremendous amount of fear. Nations all over the globe have shut down their economies for an extended period of time because of this virus, and this has caused tremendous economic suffering and great chaos all over the planet.

So it would appear that COVID-19 perfectly fits the first pandemic that John Paul Jackson saw, and that means that a more serious pandemic is coming after this one, and other prophetic voices have seen this as well.

But before I get to that, I want to talk about a man in Kentucky that was shown the COVID-19 pandemic and the great civil unrest that would erupt in the aftermath of the death of George Floyd in a prophetic experience that he had in late 2019. I learned about his testimony as I was nearly done with this book, and it is a perfect example of how God uses ordinary people in extraordinary ways.

In December 2019, Pastor Dana Coverstone of Living Word Ministries Assemblies of God in Burkesville, Kentucky had a prophetic dream that he shared with members of his church. As the events that he witnessed in his dream started happening, Pastor Coverstone and the members of his church realized the importance of what he had been given, and Pastor Coverstone decided to share it on Facebook. Since hardly anyone in the entire country had ever heard of him at that point, Pastor Coverstone didn't anticipate that a whole lot of people would see the video, but it quickly went viral. At this point the video has been viewed more than a million times, and at the time I am writing this it continues to spread all over social media like wildfire.

My wife made a transcription of his original video, and the following is an excerpt from that transcription...

Here's what happened:

Back in December I woke up, I had a dream. In that dream I saw a calendar. Starting January 2020.

It was being flipped. I saw January, I saw February, I saw March. When March came up the hand held it and I saw the thing of finger underline the month of March, and the tap it three times.

So underline the month of March, tapped it three times.

So to me it was emphasis, something's going to happen in March.

Then I saw April, May, June. When June came, the hand underlined June again and tapped it three times.

Then, in the vision I saw people marching, I saw protests. I saw people were in masks, I saw lines going into hospitals. I saw typical medical doctors with needles or syringes, I saw people on ventilators, I saw people who were very, very sick, very, very ill. I saw newspaper headlines trumpeting thousands of people getting sick. I saw ambulances, just flying down roads, and then I saw cities on fire.

I saw buildings being burned. I saw protesters with masks. I saw people who had their fists in the air, people who were yelling and screaming angry at just at the world. I saw courthouses, I saw statehouses surrounded. I saw people who were mad at the world. I saw I saw guns shotguns specifically put in the air, held like this, (showing above his head) and I saw barriers within cities.

I told several men in my church about this and I can confirm who those men were and they'll confirm what I'm telling you is what I told them.

Source: https://bit.ly/2ZgpBJD

Obviously this is a very accurate description of the COVID-19 pandemic and the horrific rioting, looting and violence that erupted in the aftermath of the death of George Floyd.

Pastor Dana was shown more about what is coming in our future in subsequent dreams, and I will be including excerpts from those dreams in later chapters in this book. Some people have been assuming that everything that he saw in those dreams will happen during this calendar year, but that is definitely not true. In fact, I believe that it is quite clear that the things that he saw in his dreams will happen over an extended period of time. Without a doubt, the chaotic events that he and others have been shown will come to pass, but it will take some time for everything to fully play out.

Many had been hoping that this coronavirus pandemic would quickly fade, but that hasn't been the case. Sadly, it has now become clear that it will be with us for a long time to come.

On July 1st, 2020, Dr. Maurice Sklar had a prophetic experience in which he was shown that things would actually get worse in the months ahead...

There's, there is a,... I don't know if it's another form of this same China virus that we've experienced, it might be a new one or it may be just a resurgence, I don't know, but I saw I saw ambulances. I saw hospitals being filled. I saw the shutdown of the schools, which are planning to open.

Source: https://bit.ly/2CqZlVq

It was not clear to Dr. Sklar what pandemic he was witnessing. It may have been a resurgence of COVID-19 or it may have been the next pandemic that is coming. But if you watch the video in which he shared this prophetic experience, you will see that what he was shown really shook him up.

The COVID-19 pandemic and the nightmarish civil unrest that we have already been witnessing have both hit the U.S. economy really hard. Tens of millions of Americans have lost their jobs, more than 100,000 businesses have shut down permanently, and vast numbers of families suddenly find themselves in need of help.

Several years ago, Heidi Baker had a vision of huge lines of people in the United States lined up to get food, and at first she really didn't know what to make of that vision. The following is what she was shown…

I had a vision in your church and it wasn't what I expected to see. I saw bread lines, soup kitchens, and I saw people wearing beautiful clothing. Their clothing was not worn out. Now in my nation when people are hungry you can tell. I mean they are in shredded rags. They don't have shoes or they have flip flops. Most of them have no shoes. They are hungry and they know they are hungry. They come for food, not because they are beggars, but because they are hungry.

I have held starving children in my arms. I know what starvation is. I know what pain is. I know what suffering is. But in this vision that I had that was in your nation, which the Lord is helping me to say, I will identify with America as well as Mozambique.

I saw this bread line, long bread lines, and I said, "Lord, I don't think that is popular to say in a church, especially one that is all about revival and victory and power."

I didn't want to see what I saw, but I saw what I saw so, I was so undone that I just said what I saw. And I saw all these people and they had beautiful cars, 4 by 4's and Lexus, Mercedes, BMW's, Toyotas. There they were with fancy shiny cars, but they were standing in line.

What I said about worrying, the worriers turned into worshipping warriors.

I asked, "Why are they so well dressed and standing in this line?"

He said, "Because it is a suddenly. They are suddenly in need of food."

Source: https://bit.ly/2XpuVuC

Needless to say, what she was shown has now happened.

As I have been documenting on my websites, there have been lines of vehicles up to two miles long at some food banks around the country. If you can believe it, in some cases it has been reported that vehicles have been lining up as early as 2 AM because people want to make sure to be able to get something for their families before the food runs out.

If you look at photographs of these very long lines, you will notice that many of the vehicles are quite expensive, and a lot of the people are wearing very nice clothes.

It is just as Heidi Baker saw. She was shown that people with nice clothes and nice vehicles would suddenly be in need of food, and that is precisely what has happened.

Unfortunately, this is just the beginning. Another pandemic is coming that is going to be much worse, and according to John Paul Jackson it is going to involve "sores on the skin"…

There is coming another pandemic. It's not the day after tomorrow but it is coming. And this one is a serious one. This pandemic – the problem is that, the first one that was coming wasn't going to be that major, and that people would kind of make light of the next one. But the next one is not going to be that light. The next one is going to be a very stunning issue and there is going to be a lot of people – I didn't see but in a way it looked like a chickenpox type of thing again or like a smallpox type of thing again, where there are sores of the skin that take place. I'm not a doctor, so I don't know what to call that. I don't know what they symptoms might be called, but there were sores on the skin that erupted because of this issue.

Monkey Pox (?)

Source: https://bit.ly/2BoZHv6

Of course those that follow my websites on a regular basis already know that John Paul Jackson is not the only prophetic voice that was warned about such things.

For example, Sonja Craighead was shown that "plagues of infectious diseases" would come and that they would "kill many"...

God has shown me terrible sickness, infections, cancers and other disease will increase in America. Plagues of infectious diseases will spread throughout America that will be resistant to what medicine has to offer. God showed me that America will have at least a few new infectious disease that has never been to our land that there will be no known cure for that will disease and kill many.

Source: https://bit.ly/3gwXi1D

And prophet Sadhu Sundar Selvaraj from India was shown that the next pandemic that is coming "will make this coronavirus look like child's play". During a very unusual supernatural experience in late 2019, God gave him a very ominous message regarding the next major outbreak...

"Another great wind is going to sweep all over the world."

And when He spoke the word "wind," it was made for me to know this. Another great wind, worse than coronavirus pandemic is going to sweep this whole world. The world is shaken with fear and trembling because of coronavirus, but the word of the Lord came to say, another, worse than coronavirus, is going to come. When that comes, it will make this coronavirus look like child's play.

Source: https://bit.ly/3c4AJh2

After what we have already been through, it is difficult to imagine another pandemic that will be far worse.

But according to Sadhu Sundar Selvaraj that is precisely what is going to happen, and like John Paul Jackson he was also shown that this next pandemic will affect the skin...

So when this great wind comes, it will sting people like a hornet's stinger. When a hornet stings a person, a person feels hot, with fire-like sensation and swelling like boils appears on their bodies. In the same manner, when this wind stings a person, that person will feel hot like fire over them, and their temperature will rise above 100°F, above 38°C. So, the feelings will be hot like fire burning all over their body, and fever will shoot up in their bodies, more than 100°F, and boils will develop all over their faces and bodies, especially in the chest area. These are the physical symptoms when this virus stings.

Now doctors and scientists will be baffled and perplexed at not being able to discover at all any medicine or vaccine for this. This morning I read in the news, a scientific report about this coronavirus, that the scientists are still trying to understand the DNA of this virus. And they say, a vaccine will still a long time away. So there is no medicine; there is no vaccine. And by that time they claim that they have found something, this hornet will come to sting. But this time, the doctors and the scientists will not be able to discover any way how this virus works, and they will not be able to discover any medicine or vaccine.

Source: https://bit.ly/3c4AJh2

Throughout this book, I will be giving you example after example of prophetic voices that have all been shown the same thing.

Of course the reason why they are all being shown the same thing is because they are all getting it from the same source.

And it isn't just in the past few years that people have been shown that great pandemics are coming. All the way back in 1979, Sarah Menet was shown a horrific pandemic in the last days that would affect the skin, and she was shown another one that would cause people to bleed from the nose, mouth, eyes and ears...

The next thing I saw was people being sick and dying. I saw this particularly in four cities: New York, Los Angeles, San Francisco and Salt Lake. The disease started by having white blisters, some the size of dimes appear on their hands, arms and face. This quickly developed into white puffy sores and blisters. People would stumble about and fall and then many died within a short time, maybe 24 hours. I also saw other people with blood coming from their nose, mouth, eyes and ears. It started like a flu virus and it spread very quickly, faster than the other white blister disease. The people who had this disease died even faster. This was more wide spread across the entire United States. There were hundreds of thousands of people stricken with these two diseases.

I knew that the diseases, and there were several different kinds, but at first primarily these two, came from small containers that had been brought into the United States. These containers were like quart jars and I was impressed that the people carrying them would just drop them on the ground in large crowds of people and the people would become infected without realizing it.

Source: https://bit.ly/2AvndGr

I know that many of you that are encountering these prophecies for the first time may not want to believe them.

But it is important to understand that these prophecies are coming from individuals with solid track records. In 2016, Sadhu Sundar Selvaraj had a supernatural experience months before election day in which he was shown that Donald Trump would become the president of the United States, and Sarah Menet was shown 9/11 decades before that horrible tragedy ever took place.

[handwritten: That was a horror of evil]

The Bible warns us that the last days will be a time of great iniquity and lawlessness, and we live at a moment in history when the nations of the world are running away from God as fast as they can.

God has sent warning after warning, and He has strongly urged the nations of the world to repent, but that has not happened.

So now God is slowly lifting His hand of protection, and things will eventually get much, much worse.

As I close this chapter, let me share with you an excerpt from a vision that Monique Bizet was given...

I could see all around me as in 360 view, and there were dead corpses everywhere, millions of dead bodies stacked as high as buildings all over, too many to bury. The number of dead bodies stacked seemed to be without end, more than I could count and as far as my eyes could see to the left and right. The stench of the bodies was overwhelming. I was astonished by the sight of them, to the point of feeling breath-

less. Their dead flesh was gray/greenish and their hair was all gone. They all seemed to have an expression of horror with their eye sockets empty and their mouths open, like empty black holes, as if they were screaming, like something had impacted them all in a very horrific way. The bodies were so severely starved that all their ribs were projecting out..

It reminded me of what the Prophet Zechariah saw – Now this will be *the plague* with which the Lord will strike all the peoples who have gone to war against Jerusalem; their flesh will rot while they stand on their feet, and their eyes will rot in their sockets, and their tongue will rot in their mouth. (Zechariah 14:12)

They survive everything

Dirty water was streaming through the dead bodies and running through the streets. The only thing I saw alive were roaches that somehow survived and I saw bugs and flies, but it was mostly roaches covering the dead bodies, flying off and then coming back.

Source: https://bit.ly/2AyDr1y

Things didn't have to turn out this way.

If we had stopped killing babies on an industrial scale, if we had stopped committing rampant sexual immorality, and if we had quit running after every other form of sin imaginable, things could have turned out very differently.

But that didn't happen.

Throughout human history, God has always given humanity choices. He has set before us life and death, blessings and curses, and He has always given us enough room to freely choose what we wanted.

In our case, we have clearly chosen death and curses, and so that is what we shall get.

The good news is that you can individually choose to make a much different choice than society as a whole is making.

Throughout human history God has also always had a Remnant, and that Remnant is rising all around us.

In Revelation 12:17, the Remnant of the last days is described as those "which keep the commandments of God, and have the testimony of Jesus Christ." Even as the world spins out of control, this Remnant will do mighty exploits, will preach the gospel to the entire world, and will move in all the power of the Holy Spirit like we haven't seen since the Book of Acts. I believe that we will be the generation that witnesses the greatest move of God in the history of the world, and I will have much more to say about this in a later chapter.

In so many ways, what we will be facing will be the worst of times, but it will also be the best of times.

Yes, the years ahead of us are going to be much more difficult than most people would dare to imagine. But that doesn't mean that your life is over. In fact, for many of you the real purpose of your life is just now being awakened.

As I stressed at the beginning of this chapter, even though I am going to be sharing some very difficult things with you, I very much intend for this to be a book of hope.

God didn't warn us about all of these things in advance so that we could wallow in fear. He wants us to understand that everything is in His hands, He wants us to have peace, and He has a job for us to do.

All of human history has been building up to a great crescendo, and we were fortunate enough to be born during this time. We were created for a purpose, and now is the time to rise up and become everything that we were created to be.

CHAPTER 2 – PROPHETS AND PROPHECY

This is a book about prophets and prophecy, and I definitely understand that there are a lot of people out there that do not believe in such things. Our society has trained us to be skeptical about the supernatural, and this is especially true when it comes to any supernatural experiences related to the Christian faith. In addition, most Christian churches in our day and time actually shun the supernatural. Even though the Bible is absolutely packed with signs, wonders, miracles, dreams, visions and revelations, most Christians today are taught that such things don't really happen anymore. That is extremely unfortunate, because the truth is that they are happening all around us.

On the other hand, there are other Christians that seem to have very little discernment and will eagerly embrace anyone that claims to be a "prophet" or a "prophetess" without asking any questions. This is extremely unfortunate as well, because there are a whole lot of frauds and charlatans running around out there.

Just like in every other era of human history, there are true prophets in our world today, and there are false prophets.

If someone claims to be a "prophet" but the things that God supposedly "told" that individual turn out to be dead wrong, stop following that person. It amazes me how some "prophets" continue to have very large followings even though they have been proven to be false over and over.

At this point, there is a very important distinction that I want to make. If someone expresses an opinion about something that turns out to be wrong, that definitely does not make someone a false prophet. What makes someone a false prophet is when an individual claims to have some sort of message that comes directly from God, but that message turns out to be inaccurate.

There is a world of difference between sharing our own personal opinions and claiming to have received some sort of divine revelation. Everyone has personal opinions that turn out to be wrong, and that is okay. Personally, I did not think that the U.S. national debt would ever hit 30 trillion dollars, but now the federal government is spending money so fast that it won't be too long before we cross that mark. That was a personal opinion of mine, and it just happened to be incorrect. ✓ Thanks to but cle- TRUMP Joe is getting it back under

But it certainly was not a "prophecy", and all of us express opinions on various matters that will happen in the future every day. It is so important for people to understand what a "prophecy" is and what a "prophecy" is not. According to Wikipedia, a "prophecy" is defined as "a message that is claimed by a prophet to have been communicated to them by a deity." In the Bible, making such claims is a very, very serious matter, and it should only be done if you have actually had a real supernatural encounter with God.

Unfortunately, we have all sorts of people running around today constantly issuing "prophecies" to the entire nation even though they haven't physically seen or heard anything. In many cases they are just "prophesying" out of their own mind, will and emotions, and sometimes they can guess right, but much of the time they end up being dead wrong.

In other cases, there are false prophets that are having real supernatural encounters, but those encounters are with the powers of darkness. For example, there are some psychics that really do tap into the supernatural realm, but the sources that they get their "information" from are very evil.

But just because there is so much going on out there that is dead wrong does not mean that we should reject everyone that is prophetic.

Sadly, that is the error that many Christians are making today. In many circles, anyone that claims to be a "prophet" is automatically labeled as a "false prophet", and that is a tragic mistake.

A lot of Christian denominations teach that prophecy ceased after the time of Christ, but that is not true at all. In fact, we find numerous examples of prophets and prophecy in operation in the Book of Acts...

Acts 11:27 – And in these days came prophets from Jerusalem unto Antioch.

Acts 13:1 – Now there were in the church that was at Antioch certain prophets and teachers; as Barnabas, and Simeon that was called Niger, and Lucius of Cyrene, and Manaen, which had been brought up with Herod the tetrarch, and Saul.

Acts 15:32 – And Judas and Silas, being prophets also themselves, exhorted the brethren with many words, and confirmed them.

Acts 21:9 – And the same man had four daughters, virgins, which did prophesy.

Acts 21:10 – And as we tarried there many days, there came down from Judaea a certain prophet, named Agabus.

Acts 19:6 – And when Paul had laid his hands upon them, the Holy Ghost came on them; and they spake with tongues, and prophesied.

And Joel chapter 2 specifically tells us that prophetic gifts will be in operation in the last days...

28 And it shall come to pass afterward, that I will pour out my spirit upon all flesh; and your sons and your daughters shall prophesy, your old men shall dream dreams, your young men shall see visions:

29 And also upon the servants and upon the handmaids in those days will I pour out my spirit.

30 And I will shew wonders in the heavens and in the earth, blood, and fire, and pillars of smoke.

If these really are the last days before the return of the Lord Jesus Christ, we should expect to see an explosion of prophetic experiences.

And as you will see throughout this book, that is precisely what we are witnessing.

Unfortunately, we are also watching the number of false prophets greatly increase as well, and this is creating a tremendous amount of confusion.

As I discussed above, many of these false prophets are not ever physically seeing or hearing anything at all. Instead, they have learned to manufacture "prophecies" out of their own mind, will and emotions, and that is something that should never, ever be done.

Of course many of these "prophecies" end up being extremely "positive" and "uplifting". Such "prophecies" are often designed to make people feel good, and they tickle the ears of those that listen to them.

And without a doubt, true prophets often prophesy positive things too, but throughout human history one of the primary purposes of true prophets has been to warn people about difficult things that are coming if repentance does not happen.

In the Bible, Jeremiah and other true prophets in ancient Israel were warning of imminent judgment, but meanwhile a whole bunch of false prophets were telling everyone that everything was going to be just fine. Sadly, we read in Jeremiah chapter 14 that the end for those false prophets was not a positive one...

13 Then said I, Ah, Lord God! behold, the prophets say unto them, Ye shall not see the sword, neither shall ye have famine; but I will give you assured peace in this place.

14 Then the Lord said unto me, The prophets prophesy lies in my name: I sent them not, neither have I commanded them, neither spake unto them: they prophesy unto you a false vision and divination, and a thing of nought, and the deceit of their heart.

15 Therefore thus saith the Lord concerning the prophets that prophesy in my name, and I sent them not, yet they say, Sword and famine shall not be in this land; By sword and famine shall those prophets be consumed.

16 And the people to whom they prophesy shall be cast out in the streets of Jerusalem because of the famine and the sword; and they shall have none to bury them, them, their wives, nor their sons, nor their daughters: for I will pour their wickedness upon them.

Yes, there are definitely some false prophets in our day that appear to be "sounding the alarm" but that are actually complete frauds.

But most of the time, false prophets try very hard to tell people exactly what they want to hear.

In particular, we are seeing a proliferation of what some have called "fortune cookie prophecies". These prophecies tend to promise that some sort of "breakthrough" or "anointing" or "financial blessing" is right around the corner, and they supposedly apply to each one of us individually. In other words, these "fortune cookie prophecies" are directed at you, me, and every other person on this planet simultaneously no matter what their circumstances might be. I know that sounds absolutely ridiculous, but people actually believe this stuff.

These sorts of false prophecies are peppered with phrases such as "great things will happen to you" and "I will bless you in this season" and "good times are ahead".

Needless to say, if great things really were happening to every man, woman and child on the entire planet, the world would not be in the giant mess that it is today.

Don't be fooled. These false prophets are not having real supernatural encounters with God. They are not physically seeing anything and they are not physically hearing anything. They have been taught that it okay to "prophesy" anything that they "feel", and they are leading multitudes of people down a very dangerous road.

With all of that being said, I cannot stress strongly enough that there are people out there that are having real supernatural encounters with God, but because there is so much other "prophetic garbage" circulating on the Internet their messages are often drowned out in all of the confusion.

For a few moments, I would like to discuss the various forms of prophetic revelation, and hopefully this will help to clarify things for a lot of people that are reading this book.

In general, I would place prophetic experiences into one of three tiers. In the first tier are what I call "visitations". People all over the globe have reported being visited by angels, and in some instances people have been visited directly by Jesus. *this matter* These visitations can happen here on Earth, but in other instances people are taken into heaven or somewhere else. Many men and women of God have reported having conversations with Jesus or with an angel just like you would have a conversation with another person. These "tier one" encounters can be extremely powerful, but they also appear to be much rarer than "tier two" or "tier three" experiences.

In the second tier are dreams and visions. Although there are distinct differences between dreams and visions, there are also quite a few similarities. For example, dreams and visions can both be very highly symbolic, and sometimes interpreting the symbols is not easy. For example, the Apostle John was given some incredible visions in the Book of Revelation, and we continue to debate the interpretation of many of those visions to this day.

But that doesn't mean that we should discount dreams and visions, because God often uses them to communicate vital information. If you want to see this in action, just look at the Book of Matthew. In the first two chapters, we are told that God spoke to Joseph three times in dreams, and in each of those three instances the Lord was giving him extremely important instructions about what needed to be done.

If the information was that important, why didn't God just send an angel to Joseph?

That is a great question, and we don't have the answer. God's ways are higher than our ways, and He doesn't make mistakes.

Obviously the dreams worked, because Joseph followed the Lord's instructions each time.

God is not always going to communicate with us in ways that we expect, but He is always going to give us what we need as long as we are truly trusting in Him.

Visions are rarer than dreams, and most visions happen while people are awake. In a typical "open vision", the room will light up and the individual having the vision will be shown events that can be seen with his or her physical eyes. There are some visions where the person is outside of the events and is watching them unfold like a movie, and there are other visions where the person having the vision actually feels like they are right in the middle of the action. In both cases, going through such an experience can be absolutely emotionally overwhelming.

On the other hand, dreams occur when people are asleep. Unfortunately, many people do not realize that God can speak to them through their dreams. In our culture, we have been trained to believe that our dreams are all completely meaningless, but that is not true at all.

Yes, sometimes dreams are just dreams, but other times God is attempting to try to communicate something very important to us.

Dreams that are spiritual in nature tend to be much more vivid and lifelike compared to other dreams. They also tend to have a very strong emotional impact on us, and they tend to be much easier to remember after they are done. In other words, they tend not to fade from memory very quickly like other dreams do.

From Genesis chapter 20 all the way through the rest of the Bible, we see example after example of God speaking to people in dreams.

He is the same God yesterday, today and forever, and without a doubt He is still speaking to us in dreams in our time.

Sadly, most churches don't want anything to do with dreams and visions today. When I was growing up, my family attended churches that did not consider dreams to have any spiritual significance at all.

So when I had very powerful dreams, I immediately dismissed them as being insignificant. Sometimes I would dream about being in a particular place at a particular moment in time, and then much later I would be stunned to realize that the scene that I had dreamed was unfolding right in front of me in real life exactly as I had dreamed it. Once in a while I would excitedly tell someone that I had dreamed what was happening in advance, but usually I would be told that it was just a case of "deja vu" and that it really didn't mean anything.

But of course those dreams did mean something.

I just didn't realize it at the time.

If a dream happens more than once, that can be a sign that it has a very important spiritual message. When I was young, I had one particular dream that kept recurring over and over again. In the dream, I was always in a very tall building looking out at the ocean. I must have been on one of the highest floors, because the view was spectacular. I was always looking out huge glass windows that stretched from the floor to the ceiling in these dreams, and I always had a very clear view of the absolutely massive tsunami that was rapidly approaching the shore. The tsunami was much taller than the building, and I knew that it was going to cause immense destruction. In my dreams, I always woke up before the tsunami hit the building.

In those days, I had absolutely no idea that people all over the world were receiving dreams and visions about colossal tsunamis that would hammer our coastlines in the last days. In later chapters, I will share many of those dreams and visions with you. As a kid, I simply assumed that the dreams I was having were just completely meaningless dreams that didn't have any relation to reality at all.

But now I know that God does speak to us through dreams and visions, and hopefully this book will help more people to start listening.

The "third tier" of prophetic experiences includes manifestations of the gifts of the Spirit such as receiving a "word of knowledge" like we read about in 1 Corinthians chapter 12. Aliss Cresswell is someone that regularly receives absolutely amazing words of knowledge about people and she says that a "word of knowledge" is when "someone is given information from the Holy Spirit about something that they would not naturally know". (https://spiritlifestyle.com/supernatural-knowledge-holy-spirit/) Often, a word of knowledge will be given to help you minister to someone that you are encountering that moment or that you will encounter later that day.

At other times, God will drop something into your bucket because you are supposed to pray for someone or because he is letting you know that something is about to happen. I can't tell you how many times God has brought someone to mind while I am praying and then I get contacted by that individual shortly thereafter. A lot of times this is God's way of confirming that a new door for ministry has been opened.

Of course God can communicate with us in other very unusual ways as well. For example, when I am praying I will often experience sharp pain in a particular location in my body for a very short period of time, and that is a sign that I am supposed to pray for healing for someone. Once in a while that turns out to be a family member or a friend, but a lot of times I never learn who I was praying for.

And that is okay. We are just here to be obedient, and we trust God to take care of the rest.

But as I discussed earlier, not everyone that claims to be a "prophet" or a "prophetess" is having real supernatural encounters.

In fact, if you sit them down and carefully listen to some of these people, they will openly admit that they never experience anything with their five senses. Instead, many of them just feel like they are "getting a word", and they will pump out paragraph after paragraph of information that God supposedly "told" them.

These days, so many Christians are using phrases such as "God showed me" and "God told me" without ever actually seeing or hearing anything.

That is a huge mistake.

It is time for the confusion to end. There really are lots of people that are being shown things by God that they can actually see with their physical eyes and hearing things from God that they can actually hear with their physical ears, and this book is packed with such examples.

And before we dive into more examples in the next chapter, I want to share a little bit about my methodology in putting this book together.

Even before I started, I realized that there was such a gigantic mountain of information that it was going to be a real challenge to organize it in a way that would be easy for readers to absorb.

I decided to group the prophecies by category, because it is so important for everyone to understand that these prophetic voices have been shown the same things over and over again through the years. The reason why there are so many parallels between these prophecies is because they all come from the same source.

Of course many of these prophecies are extremely long, and that presented another challenge. If I included the full text of a prophecy every time I quoted one, this book would likely have been over 1000 pages long and very few people have the time to read a work of such length.

In addition, I want to keep the cost of physical copies of this book low so that people will be able to afford to distribute physical copies to their families and friends.

So I made the decision to use relevant excerpts in most cases. Following each excerpt there is a link to where you can find the entire prophecy online, and that will allow you to go examine the excerpts in context if you are interested in doing so.

Some of the prophetic voices in this book you may know, while others you probably will not know. Every time I quoted a prophecy I could have also included detailed biographical information for that particular prophetic voice, but I decided that would have been much too cumbersome. Most of those that will read this book just want to get to the heart of the matter, and so I wanted to make it really easy to get through. If you are curious about learning more about the various prophetic voices quoted in this book, I definitely encourage you to do some digging, because you will find that they are truly remarkable men and women of God.

Lastly, even though I have chosen to lay out the chapters in a particular order, that does not mean that the prophecies will be fulfilled in that order.

In fact, many of the prophetic events that I will be discussing will be overlapping one another.

In addition, I want to stress that we do not know the specific timing of when these things will be fulfilled. As I discussed in the last chapter, we have already seen some remarkable prophetic fulfillments, and it appears that we are right on the precipice of a lot more fulfillments, but in the end all timing is in the hands of God.

He has a plan, He is in control, and all of these events will play out according to His timeline.

Now that I have gotten all of those initial remarks out of the way, we are finally ready to dive into the prophecies. In each chapter, I will begin with a brief summary of what the various prophetic voices have seen, and then I will share direct excerpts from their prophecies so that you can read them for yourself.

Only a very small fraction of the population is aware of these prophecies, but my hope is that this book will begin to change that. God has been warning us about the future of America for decades, and as these prophecies start to be fulfilled none of our lives will ever be the same again.

CHAPTER 3 – ECONOMIC COLLAPSE AND FAMINE

For more than a decade, I have operated a website called The Economic Collapse Blog, and for most of that time the U.S. economy was relatively stable. Of course everyone could see that our debt-fueled "prosperity" was completely and utterly unsustainable, but for many years authorities were able to prop up the system and keep all of the economic bubbles going time after time whenever a crisis started to erupt. For a while there, I was receiving quite a bit of criticism from people that were convinced that the economy would never collapse, but now that criticism has completely stopped.

The reason why the criticism has completely stopped is because the U.S. economy is now collapsing. Economic activity has fallen off dramatically, more than 100,000 businesses have permanently closed their doors, and tens of millions of Americans have lost their jobs. The numbers tell us that this is the worst economic downturn since the Great Depression of the 1930s, and unfortunately things are going to get even worse.

A lot worse.

For decades, God has been showing His people that the U.S. economy is eventually going to completely implode.

I am not talking about a "recession" or even a "depression". Ultimately we will get to a point where we won't have a functioning economy at all.

The Mother of Jesus said the U.S. will become like a third world country.

Of course a lot of things have to happen to get us to that point, and the events described in other chapters will play a major role. Natural disasters, civil unrest, political turmoil, pandemics and war will all be part of the "perfect storm" that will absolutely devastate this nation, and each new blow will just accelerate our economic problems.

Always does

John Fenn was shown that the collapse would begin when conservatives are in charge, and that is precisely what has happened. This has surprised a lot of people, because many had assumed that we would only have good times as long as a Republican was in the White House.

Sadly, what we have experienced so far is just the beginning.

In this chapter, you will see that a large number of prophetic voices have been shown that eventually things will get so bad that there will actually be famine in the United States.

As I write this chapter, the U.S. is certainly not facing famine in the short-term, but much of the rest of the world is.

Armies of locusts the size of major cities have been absolutely ravaging crops in eastern portions of Africa, across the Middle East and throughout parts of Asia. In fact, the locusts have even gotten as far as India and China. These locust swarms can travel up to 90 miles a day, and when they descend upon a farm they can literally eat everything there in as little as 30 seconds. This truly is a plague of biblical proportions, but the mainstream media never makes any sort of a spiritual connection when they report on this story.

Meanwhile, African Swine Fever has wiped out about half the pigs in China and about a quarter of the pigs on the entire globe overall. Pork is one of the primary sources of protein for many nations, and this is particularly true in Asia. To say that this has been a major disaster would be a huge understatement.

And of course COVID-19 has created an incredible amount of fear and has greatly disrupted food distribution systems all over the planet.

On top of everything else, global weather patterns have gone completely nuts and this is playing havoc with crops all over the world.

We have never seen so major threats to global food production hit us simultaneously, and this has set the stage for horrific global famines.

David Beasley is the executive director of the UN World Food Program, and he has publicly stated that we are now facing "the worst humanitarian crisis since World War Two". He is warning that famines are beginning to erupt all over the planet, and he says that we could soon see 300,000 people around the world starve to death every single day…

If we can't reach these people with the life-saving assistance they need, our analysis shows that 300,000 people could starve to death every single day over a three-month period. This does not include the increase of starvation due to COVID-19.

In a worst-case scenario, we could be looking at famine in about three dozen countries, and in fact, in 10 of these countries we already have more than one million people per country who are on the verge of starvation.

Source: https://www.wfp.org/news/wfp-chief-warns-hunger-pandemic-covid-19-spreads-statement-un-security-council

For now, the U.S. is not in danger of experiencing famine.

But we are having shortages

But that will eventually change.

As "the perfect storm" progresses, it will become increasingly difficult to produce food, and eventually there will be severe shortages.

But it will take some time for this to fully play out. At first, we will notice that food prices are rising dramatically, and John Paul Jackson has seen that there will be armed guards on food trucks.

Needless to say, this will help to fuel the tremendous civil unrest that I am going to talk about in another chapter, and people will become increasingly desperate.

Eventually, there simply will not be enough food for everyone, and we will see starvation in the United States of America.

In the Bible, it took two or three witnesses to establish a matter. But rather than just share two or three examples in each chapter, I have decided to flood you with examples of prophetic voices that all confirm one another.

Over the past 50 years, God has warned us over and over and over again that these things were coming, and yet only a very small sliver of the population has been willing to listen.

The reason why these prophetic experiences have all been so remarkably consistent over the last 50 years is because they all came from the same source.

God is trying to get our attention, and my hope is that this book will bring more attention to these prophecies than ever before.

With all that being said, here is what various prophetic voices have been shown regarding economic collapse and famine…

David Wilkerson

Investment markets around the world, oil cartels, multinational corporations, and all others will be thrown into a state of helpless bewilderment and economic confusion. The stock market will plunge again. This nation is headed for runaway inflation… What worked before to take the steam out of inflation will this time only be fuel for the fire. *And there is little a president can actually do about inflation*

A second judgment zone will be stricken with drought. Long, tragic drought. Rivers and streams will dry up. Water tables will no longer support irrigation systems. Crops will wither and die in the fields. Winds will carry away topsoil, and this nation will suffer its worst dust bowl in all its history.

The threat of major food shortage in the United States will cause a wave of hoarding. Flour, dried foods, sugar, rice, beans, and canned foods will skyrocket in price. Supermarket shelves will be emptied of staple items. The price of dried foods will eventually quadruple. People will be prepared to kill in defense of their hoarded food supplies. Prayer meetings and days and weeks of prayer will not break this drought. God will not permit unrepentant men to escape judgment by simple mouthing meaningless calls for relief. This drought will fall upon the just and unjust. Everyone's lifestyle will be affected.

Source: https://bit.ly/2yIPJUq

Nita Johnson

I saw ministers and ministries, both large and small, well known and basically unknown, go under. Ministers by the thousands left the call hoping to find stability in the world, thinking they could use their gifts and talents to make a living at a secular job. It was a heart-breaking and cataclysmic economic collapse. I was given the scripture John 10:12 – "But he that is an hireling, and not the shepherd, whose own the sheep are not, seeth the wolf [Satan] coming, and leaveth the sheep, and fleeth: and the wolf catcheth them, and scattereth the sheep."

Businesses, large and small, went under. The whole world was in upheaval. People were killing themselves over their severe losses. Families were losing homes, cars, and furniture because they hadn't prepared.

Source: https://bit.ly/3eSEQPe

Daniel Rodes

I saw the stock market fluctuate up and down and finally come to a complete crash, never to rise again. There will be an extreme shortage of food, drinking water, and many people will die of starvation. The Word of the Lord came to me and said, "Because prosperity and pleasure has become the god of America, she shall suffer the consequences of her rejection against Me."

Source: https://bit.ly/3cmDwm4

John Fenn

As happens so often, it is a combination of things in the natural and things spiritual coming together that turn a person's heart towards me. The collapse will come when conservatives are in charge, and they will be blamed for the nation's ills, though what will happen is actually the result of poor decisions made by many before them.

Source: https://bit.ly/2MmV5b6

It always happens under Republican charge. They always take care of the rich & hurt the poor or middle class. They are full of greed. All you have to do is look at their pattern & history.

A Prophetic Vision Given To Jerry Golden In 2001

There were fires and explosions all over the city and people were running in total panic. There were wrecked cars and cabs on nearly every street, and there were soldiers everywhere I looked. I felt a Holy Presence but could not see anyone. I asked if this was the World Trade Center we had just seen on TV, and He said "No, this is yet to come." I then asked if it would only be New York City? He said, "No, many others will suffer in even worse ways. In other cities there will be death and destruction across the United States. The economy will be totally destroyed and when their god of money is gone from them, they will turn to me. But I will receive them not."

Source: https://bit.ly/2Mhn7EW

Commodities Broker Steve Meyers

We will have a food crisis that will cause mass food shortages. Droughts, floods, the disease will cut the food supply and many people will suffer starvation. I saw trade wars that would lead to shooting wars and, this is worldwide but primarily centered in the middle east. One day I'm watching the markets and stocks, bonds, and dollar collapse at the same time. No bids. It was breathtaking. I could feel the fear of knowing the implications almost immediately. On the other side, the price of gold was shooting up so incredibly fast that it was equally unnerving. We have never witnessed or experienced such chaos in our lives. Prices soar out of control for everyday items. People were screaming out for all the madness to stop. People starving. Freedoms lost as the government took total control. Marshall Law etc. As I described the events to my friend immediately following the vision, the words I used were, "It is going to resemble a Mad Max movie."

Source: https://bit.ly/3eIGt26

Monique Bizet

There was an economic collapse that took place greater than the magnitude of Great Depression. A time of great refining for the Christians, great suffering and enduring until the end.

Source: https://bit.ly/31Ey8ZV

Glynda Lomax

It was late Saturday night, February 9th, 2019, and I was doing some computer and paperwork in front of the television when a commercial of some kind came on and there was a clip in it having to do with economics. And I saw a flash vision.

I saw the economy had crashed and it kept going lower and lower and lower and I heard this great silence. And I heard over and over "Something is missing. Something is missing."

I kept asking Why is it crashing, Lord? But all I heard was "Something is missing."

Well, Lord, for sure YOU are missing from most people's lives.

I saw factories grind to a standstill. I saw Not Hiring signs going up on fast food places. I saw husbands and wives fighting over spending and trying to cut costs.

I saw that food prices were astronomical. They are already so high, but I saw prices so high people could barely buy two items.

Source: https://bit.ly/3cQE049

Sarah Menet

The next thing that I felt more than I saw was that shortly after this there was no commerce, no shopping, buying, and was impressed that there was no economy. The economy had almost failed completely and no one had any money.

Source: https://bit.ly/2XNNdpJ

John Paul Jackson

He said, "Begin to watch the European Community because I'm going to trouble the waters in Europe and the Euro is going to start to fall. And it will weaken and it will crumble. And shortly after that, your dollar will follow."

Source: https://bit.ly/2YnVRKo

Pastor Shane Warren

In 2011 I was watching television and it turned into a vision of the future. A weather broadcast appeared and the news anchor said, "The most amazing thing is going on right now. It's tragic … It's tragic." Normally hurricanes hit on the coastal lines, he said, but there is a hurricane that is spreading across America." He showed a satellite image of America, a storm covering from north, south and from east to west over America.

The scene changed to a news reporter in the eye of the storm, the wind is blowing violently, and He said, "This is amazing. This is not a natural storm. This isn't normal, it's raining; and he reached down and picked up a fist full of dollar bills. It's raining dollar bills. It's almost like they're worthless. They're worthless. It was raining worthless dollars."

Source: https://bit.ly/3cX0dgQ

Pastor Dana Coverstone

In this dream we just had a yard sale to help fund a team going to Ecuador this next year.

We had a yard sale. I had asked our secretary to get some change for that for that yard sale. So, in the dream that I'm having, I walk to the bank. I walk into the bank to get some change. On the door, it says there's no change available.

I saw the sign and registered in mind. I walked on in, and the president of the local bank was at the teller station. She was taking care of business.

And I said, I need to get $10 in quarters for yard sale and she said, I'm sorry, but the US Mint is no longer making currency or making change... (like pennies nickels dimes quarters half dollars), "We're not doing that anymore".

"Well what do you mean?"

She said, ... "they stopped doing it".

I said, "Well, how am I going to be able to charge $1.50 for anything?"

She said, "prepare for hyperinflation and just charge $2".

Then she said to me in the dream... Oh by the way, $1 and $5 bills will follow soon after that.

Then I heard those words. "Brace yourself. Brace yourself. Brace yourself."

Source: https://bit.ly/2ZgpBJD

Mary Ann Brown's 1976 Vision

I saw food lines as far as the eye could see: food will begin to dwindle, because of no rain and floods. It will be a difficult time, men will go wild because of a spirit to survive: Anger – Riots – Murder. People will fear to come out of their houses.

Source: https://bit.ly/2XZxtjw

Daisy Osborn

'In a VISION' I saw: the face of the earth and the changing of the shape of America. It was drastically altered and reduced in size through terrible disasters. Hunger and suffering were every-where. The devastation caused by volcanic eruptions and fires were widespread and horrifying during this terrible holocaust.

Source: https://bit.ly/2AYEkAx

Dr. Roxanne Brant's 1973 Vision

The only things worth having were land, food, seed, wood for fuel, a home that was not mortgaged, farming tools and machin-ery, and certain everyday products which were no longer avail-able. Many people simply left their jobs and tried to grow enough food to live on. Many of our largest and most trusted corporations went bankrupt. Many valuable machines were setting idle because they lacked the one necessary part to fix them. Many people who were living beyond their means and who had mortgages on their homes were turned out into the streets. Insolvable problems presented themselves in every area, in politics, as well as economics and weather. There were so many quick changes, that by the time we had heard of one change, another change had already occurred.

Source: https://bit.ly/37s7Vyh

Sonja Craighead

God specifically showed me that we were living in a time of illusion of great prosperity but that will not last. Our nation will fall into great debt. This short-lived illusion prosperity will happen regardless who who is our president. God showed me that the financial losses will be so monumental that America will not be able to financially recover from the soon coming catastrophic financial losses.

Source: https://bit.ly/3gwXi1D

Evangelist Joan Schmitz

Vision 1: While in intercession in the Spring of 1973, I received two visions. What I saw and heard I now write, as the Lord has confirmed that this is His time for me to write them down, for they are for the Body of Christ.

Scene 1 — As the vision opened I saw myself digging in a garbage bag. This so surprised me that out of my spirit I said, "Lord, what am I doing digging in a garbage bag?" It was then that a man appeared before me. He was skin and bones, having hollow eyes. The Lord spoke into my spirit — "FAMINE."

Scene 2 — The next scene that came before me was a street scene. The atmosphere was somewhat dark, but I could see people gathered on the corner. At this point I was made aware that there was fighting and great turmoil. It was then the Lord spoke in my spirit that "many would die by the sword and famine."

Scene 3 — In the next scene I was lifted up by the Spirit, and as I was looking down, I saw people marching in ranks. Their appearance was that of starvation, as they were skin and bones with hollow eyes. As I watched and listened, into my spirit I was reminded of the great persecution of the Jews under Hitler during World War II. As they marched they were singing a song in a language that I was not familiar with. As I listened, I began to sing in the Spirit the same song. At a later time, the Lord showed me that this would be the coming persecution of the Church and the Jews. It was then that the Lord spoke to me saying, "The stage is being set and the curtain is about to rise on the whole new world system, and the money you have will not be worth the paper it's written on."

Source: https://bit.ly/30eaXVm

Hollie L. Moody

"What about my nation, Lord?" I asked. "What is coming next to my nation (The United States of America)?"

"A measure of wheat for a penny, and three measures of barley for a penny; and see thou hurt not the oil and the wine," the Lord replied softly. "Economic lack is coming to your nation," the Lord said to me.

"There are some I will and have begun to instruct to lay up and store certain food, water household and medical supplies. There are others I have instructed to trust in Me daily for their needs, and to refrain from storing up supplies. Nothing will remain stable in your nation for any length of time, child. This ever present uncertainty will cause many to grow weary. A spirit and attitude of quiet despair will begin to prevail. This lassitude will begin to set in place the next area of attack from the enemy."

Source: https://bit.ly/2As5RdA

Dr. Roxanne Brant's 1973 Vision

But most of the country and world would be under the super-natural siege of God with ever increasing and worsening droughts, flooding, earthquakes, storms, tornadoes, hurricanes, pestilence, etc. I knew that because of these natural judgments of God that many crops would fail and millions of people in different places of the United States and the world would be starving. It is not a pretty picture and is therefore very difficult for me to talk about, but I saw millions of people starving and trying to find edible roots and grasses to eat. I saw presidents of corporations reduced to nothing except their homes and the food in their cupboards. One man was trying to warm watery soup for his family on a fire in his backyard.

Source: https://bit.ly/37s7Vyh

David Wilkerson

Before the great holocaust, there will be smaller holocausts – the oil fields of the middle east will be ablaze, and the smoke will rise night and day as a warning of the greater holocaust yet to come. There will be bombs falling on oil fields, on shipping docks and storage tanks. There will be panic among all oil pro-ducers, and shippers, and upon all nations dependent on that oil.

Source: https://bit.ly/2A4cUcy

Sean Harper

He spoke in a booming concerned voice, "This shall be a sign unto you. When you see a major jump and attack on oil. Know the children with be left to tread open water with the blood-thirsty sharks. They will not escape."

Source: https://bit.ly/2ANgB6p

We need to get rid of our dependence on fossil fuels.

Sonja Craighead

I saw in the Midwest states of Iowa, Ohio and parts of Missouri corn standing in mud and water being ruined by flooding with rot and mold on the corn ears.

I saw freezes and frost in Georgia and Florida damaging most of their fruit Citrus crops.

In California I saw even more severe drought conditions the ground was actually cracking and breaking to the point that many farmers didn't bother even to plant new vegetable crops knowing that they hadn't enough irrigation water to bring their crops to harvest.

Source: https://bit.ly/3gwXi1D

Dr. Maurice Sklar

People were starving, they had no food, there was looting, and gangs were going about, …it was just awful. People were starving.

Source: https://bit.ly/2TCTEta

Michelle Walcott

People were growing food in their homes/basements because it was not safe to do so outside, not sure why. Perhaps the food could be stolen or poisoned?

I visited a friend in this part of the dream who I used to work with. He took me in his basement and he had rows of garden tables with veggies under lights. He had the juiciest looking tomatoes.He told me it wasn't safe to grow them outside but he didn't say why.

Source: https://bit.ly/2X0InET

Sonja Craighead

God has told me to warn His people living in the US that famine, both of the word of God, and a famine of not enough to eat, is surely coming soon to America and it's going to be severe.

He also showed me that much of the food that Americans will have in the near future will not be safe to eat for more than one reason.

In a vision from the Lord, I saw food that was beautiful to look at but unsafe to consume. (Radiation?)

Source: https://bit.ly/3gwXi1D

John Paul Jackson

Drought is going to continue to escalate in the lower half of the United States. So much so, just as it says in Revelations Chapter 6, A loaf of bread...there may be bread but what it is going to cost you will be enormous. So much so they will have to put guards on trucks to keep trucks from being robbed for their food.

Source: https://bit.ly/2YnVRKo

Sarah Menet

There was a tremendously long winter that lasted into summer. It caught everyone by surprise and started the full famine. Actually, I realized that the long winter actually just increased the famine greatly to its full measure, because the famine had already been in progress because of the storms, droughts, floods and other plagues that had been happening over the few years leading up to the long winter.

It seemed then that the year following the long winter was when everything started to go down hill very quickly or things piled up one on top of the other without any breaks. The sense of time though was not very clear because I was seeing several things that seemed to happen all at the same time or very close together.

Source: https://bit.ly/2XNNdpJ

Katie Troutman

These were good people, men in office attire with their shirts hanging out. They were just worn out looking, shaking and disoriented. They looked tired and so hopeless. They walked the streets, thousands upon thousands of them. There were no words to describe the despair. It was unimaginable.

There were gas stations open. I was riding in a truck and was just observing everything and everyone. No one was giving food out. Everyone was fending for themselves. This mass of people were all homeless and it was like I was just there in the middle of it all, watching them all night long. As I watched them wandering, I saw their depression and sadness. Our world was a much different place.

Source: https://bit.ly/2MxCCbR

Sonja Craighead

People were in a state of panic. Many people were stealing what food they could find. People began hoarding and hiding food. Many people were stealing food from their neighbors, strangers and even their own family members just to find something to eat. I saw these things happening during each crops growing cycle for a period of 2 years. The losses were so intense and there were severe shortages. After two years America was in a very severe famine.

Source: https://bit.ly/3gwXi1D

Brother Heath

Anarchy and bloodshed, hunger and starvation, people killing people over dwindling food resources. Neighbor was against neighbor, brother against brother, children against their parents, betrayal and horrific atrocities perpetrated over food and water supplies. Mobs of people grouped together ransacking, pillaging and murdering the confused and battered population. It seemed everyone was desperate, without natural affection or compassion. The stronger survivalists preyed on the weak, treating others like zombies and would kill them, along with their children and even babies without batting an eye. Foreign soldiers took part in the terror. The atrocities were worse than any Hollywood apocalyptic portayal with some lawless ones even resorting to cannabalism, like wolves, eating from dead corpses.

Source: https://bit.ly/37kvGbT

CHAPTER 4 – CIVIL UNREST AND MARTIAL LAW

Fox news & other conservative programming teaching hate.

For years we have been watching anger, frustration and hatred rise to very dangerous levels in America, and for years I have been warning that great civil unrest was coming. In fact, if you go to any of my websites and do a search for "civil unrest", you will get page after page of articles. And as you will see below, over the past 50 years many prophetic voices have also been warning that great civil unrest was coming. Of course now it seems quite obvious that there will be great turmoil in this nation, because many of the protests that erupted in the aftermath of George Floyd's tragic death were marred by tremendous violence. We have witnessed widespread rioting, looting and chaos in major cities all over the nation, and things are so tense that more violence could erupt at literally any moment.

I have been so deeply saddened by what we have been witnessing, because this should be a moment when our country is coming together, but instead it is being torn apart. In my last book, I spent an entire chapter denouncing the evils of racism, and there is certainly no place for it in our society. Of course neither should there be any place for the rioting, looting and violence that we have seen. As I have warned countless times, if we don't learn how to love one another we simply are not going to make it as a nation.

Unfortunately, the mainstream media and many of our polit-

Conservative media

49

ical leaders are constantly stirring up more strife, discord, hatred and division. No matter what happens in the news, we have been trained to pick a side and to hate those that are on the other side.

For example, for conservatives it can be so easy to hate someone like Nancy Pelosi. But whenever we look at someone, we should see someone that Christ deeply loves. In fact, Jesus loves Nancy Pelosi so much that he died on the cross for her.

Even if we disagree with every single thing that some politician says and does, we should still love that person and pray for that person.

Ultimately, love is the answer, but voices such as mine are being greatly drowned out by all of the hateful voices in our society.

So a lot more civil unrest is coming, and as you will see below, eventually this will result in martial law being declared in at least some of our major cities.

On the morning of June 21st, 2020 I had a dream about this unrest. I was in a major U.S. city, and I had just attended a gathering where voices from the community were permitted to give their perspective on the tremendous civil unrest that was happening. I was given the chance to speak too, and I denounced both racism and the violence that we were seeing all around us. And like I just shared in this chapter, I spoke about how love is the ultimate answer to our problems. Following the meeting, I spotted a very angry older white man walking behind me in a shopping mall. He had a knife pulled out and he threatened to kill me. He was extremely upset about what I had said for some reason, but fortunately I was fast enough to get away from him. Later on I went to find my vehicle, but I noticed that the same very angry older white man and a very angry older white woman were waiting near my vehicle to ambush me. I decided to abandon my vehicle and find another way home, and so they were never able to get to me. But what struck me more than anything else in the dream was the intense hatred that I felt all around me.

In all my years, I have never seen as much hatred in America as I am seeing today, and the economic collapse that I discussed in the last chapter is only going to intensify societal tensions.

In late June, Pastor Dana Coverstone had a dream in which he also saw that this nation is on the verge of tremendous civil unrest. This is what he was shown...

Here's what I saw.

I saw a calendar. Start with the calendar. As I was having this, the calendar was up, a white figure appeared. To me, it was a representing God the Holy Spirit, something pure, something righteous, something true, something Holy because there was nothing sinister about it. Nothing evil, but I heard the voice say, "part two, part two".

I saw June, go, I saw July. I saw August, and then I saw September, and I saw the finger underneath the word September and I like like emphasizing it and tap the three times.

Then I saw October come up, and then I saw November and this is when it got real to me in the dream. I think the intensity for me... when I woke up my heart rate was about 180.

So that was Monday night, and I woke up not feeling very well at all I was up during the night not feeling well.

But anyway,.... The minute the finger underlined November three times instead of tapping it, I saw a fist ball up and it hit the calendar.

And literally, the calendar exploded into the wall, the numbers seem that they were 3d and they were falling everywhere.

There was a cloud of chaos that started in there. The next thing I saw was I saw I saw armed protesters. I saw fighting in the streets, I saw people pummeling one another. I saw businesses shuttered and shut up.

I saw schools close. I saw school rooms with cobwebs hanging in them and like things like papers falling off the wall and posters... like no one had been in them for months.

I saw banks. Bank buildings with the roof being taken off. It looked almost that alien abduction because money was flying through the roof into some type of like a vacuum cleaner. It sounds kind of strange, but I was watching wealth, just being taken. I saw politicians in back rooms, making deals with people. Patting people on the back and laughing and smiling and smirking.

I saw monuments. I saw Washington DC, burning. I saw Washington DC blazing. I saw fires, everywhere.

Source: https://bit.ly/2ZgpBJD

There has been a lot of confusion about Pastor Coverstone's dreams, and I hope that people can understand that everything that he saw in this particular dream will not happen by November or even by the end of the year. I believe that events will certainly escalate as we approach the end of 2020, but the tremendous chaos that he witnessed will stretch out over a period of years.

We are going to see things happen in this country that we have never seen before, and the violence is going to shock the entire planet.

But none of this should be a surprise to us, because prophetic voices have been warning us for decades that this was coming...

David Wilkerson

For ten years I have been warning about a thousand fires coming to New York City. It will engulf the whole megaplex, including areas of New Jersey and Connecticut. Major cities all across America will experience riots and blazing fires—such as we saw in Watts, Los Angeles, years ago.

There will be riots and fires in cities worldwide. There will be looting—including Times Square, New York City.

Source: https://bit.ly/2YnOG6S

Pastor Shane Warren

I saw riots break out in major cities all over America. People were rioting in the streets and on their signs was written, "Give us our entitlements ... Give us our entitlements." I saw great demonstrations and violence in the streets whenever these different things are lost, because there's not enough money to keep up the subsidies. → *This could happen if Republicans get their way & do away with Social Security & Medicare. That is our money.*

Source: https://bit.ly/3cXOdgQ

John Paul Jackson

There is anger going to be erupting. There is violence going to be in the streets. Rich houses and neighborhoods are going to be invaded. The Robin Hood mentality, "What's yours is mine," is going to spread and all you're going to be seeing in [some] multimillion dollar neighborhoods is chimneys left standing and burnt chars of the houses. Violence is going to be so prevalent that police forces are not going to be able to take care of it. And even the military forces will only be able to take care of it in the urban areas and not the rural areas. Not even all the urban areas will be taken care of. It will be so wide spread.

Source: https://bit.ly/2YnVRKo

Marty Breeden

I saw inner cities blazing with fires and teams of gangs of all races and creeds and ethnicities banding together. This scene appears as though it is night time, although my experiences have only happened during the day.

Then I was ushered hours ahead to see the results of their rioting and looting and violence, and their effect on the land they trampled on and left behind. The land was grey and flat and desolate with burning cars, burning buildings, and ashes. Men and women were wearing bandanas and masks to hide their faces. They formed gangs and were carrying firearms and clubs and machetes with a viciousness and a blood thirst that was not human. It was pure demonic!!

Source: https://bit.ly/37u8WWW

Monique Bizet

Nov 10, 2018 I heard the Lord say Judgment is coming, the nation will be judged, He said it twice very distinct with great authority and very sternly. It certainly got my attention.

The Lord said there are tsunami waves of hatred coming upon the nation to divide it even more between all kinds of groups. There is going to be intimidation, fear tactics, to seek to manipulate and control population.

Source: https://bit.ly/2NPpeAJ

Augusto Perez

Gangs with guns were looting and pillaging everything; people were killing each other for food and water to feed their children and family. The famine was so great, that people became cannibals. The police had become militarized and very violent, beating and shooting people, taking them to FEMA camps, separating them from their children. The screams of the people is something I will never forget.

I can still hear the blood curdling screams of the people as they fled in horror for their lives. The things that I saw were so graphic, that I am not able to share them. It was such a horrific experience, that every time I remember the things that I saw, it causes me pain.

Source: https://bit.ly/3dPDZPe

David Wilkerson

There will be unbelievable, unnecessary, uncontrollable violence. The violence that had been seething beneath the surface for years will explode. No city street will be safe. The aftermath of it all is an outbreak of raping, murdering, and burning.

Source: https://bit.ly/2M778cw

Mary Ann Brown's 1976 Vision

I saw Dallas, Houston, San Antonio, New Orleans, Baton Rouge, San Francisco, Los Angeles, San Diego, Washington State, Washington D.C., Boston, Newark, New York City, Nashville, Little Rock on fire. cities burning. St. Louis on fire.

Source: https://bit.ly/2XZxtjw

Marty Breeden

April 5, 2020 Dream

As I just took a very brief nap, I had a very short "flash dream".
I've seen this same scenario in a past dream.

I saw many of our large metropolitan areas in complete and total chaos.
It was absolute insanity!

Rogue gangs banding together and creating ABSOLUTE havoc!!
Looting, rioting, murdering....
People running for their lives.

I saw great fires on both large and small buildings.
The violence was staggering to my mind.
I think about the words of Jesus in Matthew 24:37:
"But as the days of Noah were, so shall also the coming of the Son of man be!"

What did the days of Noah look like?
We are told in Genesis 6:13:
"And God said to Noah, "The end of all flesh has come before Me, for the earth is filled with violence through them;"

My friends...we are indeed in very dark and desparate times, but they are about to get even darker and MORE desperate!

Stay prepared, ...Be strong in the Lord and the power of His might and make yourself ready to defend your family and your-self!!!

Source: https://bit.ly/2AzuV1W

Elane Durham

Country Living.

And I saw that because of the ramifications of these day-to-day choices the people, especially on the eastern side of this new body of water, lived in great danger and fear. There was tremendous anarchy and crime — sort of like the Los Angeles riots spread nationwide. And the normal citizens kept themselves hidden away from all this, barricading themselves into their homes or wherever they had gathered together for security. Many children didn't go to school; commerce as we know it had pretty much ceased; many people were starving to death; there was terrible violence from people who seemed like roving gangs — it was just an awful scene of confusion and turmoil.

Source: https://bit.ly/3hofmLG

David Wilkerson

There's going to be fear like we've never known, judgment at the door. When I was at Macy's Department store in a vision and I watched people walking around stunned, they didn't know what to do, they didn't know what was happening. Then a bunch of people walked into Macy's and suddenly went wild and began to steal, and within an hour everybody, I saw the spirit of everybody in the store, they were robbing and stealing, they raped Macy's and destroyed five floors. Macy's was raped and ruined in a period of an hour or two.

Source: https://bit.ly/2XQh28N

Mary Ann Brown's 1976 Vision

I saw riots, chaos, murder, lack of food, people will be like animals. It will make room for the One World Government, the One World Money, and the One World Church. The Antichrist spirit will be behind it. I saw government, civilians, military and churches being moved. Make room for the Antichrist – in the midst of desperation, depression and lawlessness.

Source: https://bit.ly/2XZxtjw

Dr. Maurice Sklar

There was widespread looting and gangs roaming about every-where with guns, stealing whatever food and supplies they could find.

Source: https://bit.ly/2AjCutu

Commodities Broker Steve Meyers

I saw random violence much as we have already seen but believe me, we haven't seen anything yet. Safe places (or what we think of safe places) like grocery stores or clothing stores will become places of mass killings through shootings or bombings. Confusion and terror reign. Truth disappears. The Lord clearly told me there is no escape. We can't pick up and move to Costa Rica for instance because this is a spiritual battle that is being waged. Evil will be unleashed. Demonic forces will be every-where.

[handwritten note: Already happened]

Source: https://bit.ly/3eIGt26

Michelle Walcott

All of a sudden I looked up and saw a couple of men dressed all in black with a strange looking sort of hat on their head, like a Beret' I suppose but that wasn't so clear. What was clear is that these were not our Military but some sort of group that was there because Martial law had been declared in the USA. I didn't know why in the dream but I knew in my spirit in the dream that we were now under Martial law.

Source: https://bit.ly/2X0InET

Sonja Craighead

I saw extreme poverty, crime, fear, violence and unrest like our nation has never seen before. The riots looting and theft that we have seen in the past on TV news will seem mild compared to what will be in the future.

People will feel like they have nothing to lose because they're so desperate scared hungry and angry.

Anger, rage, violence and fear will be throughout our country. The viciousness and violence of mobs of people that I saw is hard for me to put even put into words. It was like they had no conscience. It was like a wounded wild animalistic behavior. It will be unsafe both in American cities as well as our picturesque countrysides.

Source: https://bit.ly/3gwXi1D

Brother Heath

After this I saw large crowds of protesters clashing in violence and bloodshed. A fire from a huge street brawl in Washington DC suddenly exploded and the flames were propelled in every direction across the nation. Raging fires, anarchy and violence could be seen from coast to coast. I then saw a news broadcast with the blurry but readable headline "Martial Law" and then the words "Civil Unrest" but as I focused on the title more closely it morphed into the words "Civil War".

Source: https://bit.ly/3dGBYEN

Sarah Menet

As these people were fleeing the cities, there were gangs attacking them and killing them. In the cities that were struck with the disease, there was complete chaos, looting, rioting, murdering, a complete breakdown. Many people seemed to go absolutely crazy. I sensed that the electricity had failed everywhere now and that nothing was running, there was no communication or anything anywhere in the country. Nothing worked, no radios or TVs. I watched people throw rocks and break windows to steal TVs which I thought was really crazy because they wouldn't work.

Source: https://bit.ly/2XNNdpJ

Sonja Craighead

An internal war will take place first. Mobs of people will roam, rob, brutalize, murder, set fires. The hatred and rage of all these roving mobs are beyond human explanation, and they are demonic with intense hatred.

Source: https://bit.ly/3gwXi1D

Peter Michael Martinez

I sensed the evil that was keeping the cities dark was meant to cause the death of millions of people. People were dying of everything from disease, to toxic fumes, to violence. Society was disintegrating and no one seemed to care. The dead bodies were everywhere, but not for long. There were what I call slaves who were charged with picking up the dead. It seemed they did this every day.

Source: https://bit.ly/2UC2B6A

Sarah Menet

Some of the people seemed to go crazy and went around in gangs killing people just for the sake of killing. Others killed for food or for things but the people who killed just to kill were absolutely terrible. They seemed like beasts, animals completely out of control as they raped, looted, burned and butchered people. I saw them go into people's homes and drag families out who were hiding there and rape them and butcher them.

Source: https://bit.ly/2XNNdpJ

CHAPTER 5 – THE COMING NEW MADRID EARTHQUAKE

For many years, I have been warning that someday there will be a catastrophic earthquake along the New Madrid fault that will rip the United States in half from the Great Lakes all the way down to the Gulf of Mexico. This enormous seismic event will actually create a new body of water in the middle of the nation, and travel across that body of water by vehicle won't be possible because all of the existing bridges and roads going from east to west across the New Madrid fault will be destroyed.

Right now, small earthquakes are occurring along the New Madrid fault quite frequently, and a large one could literally happen at any moment. But as you will see in this chapter, God has been showing people for a very long time that the catastrophic quake that will divide America in two will not happen until the United States is directly involved in officially dividing the land of Israel. At some point there will be some sort of a peace agreement which will result in the land of Israel being formally divided, and once that happens you will not want to be anywhere near the New Madrid fault.

However, I should make it very clear that we do not know how soon after the division of the land of Israel this catastrophic earthquake will happen. It could be days, it could be weeks, it could be months, or it could even be years.

But it will happen.

Sadly, most Americans do not even realize that this threat exists.

Scientists tell us that the New Madrid fault zone sits directly above a very deep geological scar, and that scar makes that part of the country geologically weaker than much of the rest of the country.

The San Andreas fault zone gets much more publicity, and I will certainly be talking about future seismic activity on the west coast in a later chapter, but the New Madrid fault zone is actually six times larger. It covers parts of Illinois, Indiana, Ohio, Missouri, Arkansas, Kentucky, Tennessee and Mississippi, and there are 15 nuclear power facilities in the region.

So when a massive seismic event hits that area, we could potentially be facing Fukushima times 15.

And such quakes have happened before. In fact, the biggest earthquakes in the history of the lower 48 states have happened along the New Madrid fault zone.

In 1811 and 1812, four enormous quakes in the region opened up very deep fissures in the ground, they were felt as far away as Washington D.C. and Boston, and they caused the Mississippi River to actually run backwards in certain places.

The following is a quote from a Smithsonian.com article about these earthquakes, and I want you to imagine what such an event would mean for the region today...

The Midwest was sparsely populated, and deaths were few. But 8-year-old Godfrey Lesieur saw the ground "rolling in waves." Michael Braunm observed the river suddenly rise up "like a great loaf of bread to the height of many feet." Sections of riverbed below the Mississippi rose so high that part of the river ran backward. Thousands of fissures ripped open fields, and geysers burst from the earth, spewing sand, water, mud and coal high into the air.

Source: https://www.smithsonianmag.com/science-nature/the-great-midwest-earthquake-of-1811-46342/

Scientists tell us that it is just a matter of time before more earthquakes like that happen again, but the truth is that what we will eventually be facing will be much worse.

Just check out what the prophetic voices have been saying over the years...

Pastor Shane Warren

Then the scene changed back to the anchor. He said, Ladies and gentlemen, another tragedy has just hit America. The New Madrid Fault, in the heartland of America has just had a major earthquake! Immediately devastation was shown all over the heartland of America, along the New Madrid Fault as earthquakes caused entire cities to crumble. And I heard a booming voice speak from behind me saying, "They have divided my land; now I will divide their land." In the vision I knew that he was speaking about Israel and specifically Jerusalem.

Source: https://bit.ly/3cX0dgQ

Dr. Maurice Sklar

The first thing I saw was America split in two, just right down the middle. It was just along the Mississippi, or just near there. It just split, like it cracked.

Source: https://bit.ly/2TCTEta

Monique Bizet

In 2015, The Lord showed me a vision that impacted me. It was so vivid. I saw a map of the USA, and then I saw Jesus standing behind the map and He said, "When the US divides My Holy Land, I will divide this land."

When He said that, I saw Him grab the map of the US and with His hands He tore the map in two; right down the middle, as you would tear a piece of paper.

I was impacted when I saw this because of all the news we have been hearing to split the Holy Land and to bring forth a two state solution under the guise of a "peace agreement."

Source: https://bit.ly/3cxFQGU

John Paul Jackson

Earthquakes will not only strike coastal areas but even in the Midwestern United States.

Source: https://bit.ly/2YnVRKo

Pastor John Kilpatrick

In this dream I knew I was experiencing a massive earthquake. The sounds were so catastrophic that the thought crossed my mind that the devastation could likely exceed Hurricane Katrina of 2005. I did not see the devastation behind me; I only heard it. In all of my life I have never heard such catastrophic sounds. These were the scariest sounds I have ever heard.

The dream then shifted once more and concluded with two names on what appeared to be an old Spanish map. One name read Indianola and the other Europa. When I awoke, I was shaking as if I had chills and a fever. I could not stop trembling. All through the day I felt as if I had just had the dream 10 minutes ago.

This dream so shook me that my wife and I immediately went to the internet to do some research. I also contacted some close friends in the ministry and reliable intercessors concerning this dream. What we found was startling. There are towns called Indianola, IL; Europa, MO; and Indianola, MS. These towns run in a line from North to South with Europa, MO being near the middle of them. The Mississippi River runs between them with Europa, MO being by the epicenter of the New Madrid fault.

Source: https://bit.ly/2YuSgub

Augusto Perez

I was in the City of Chicago when I felt a big earthquake. All the people were very scared and panicked at what was happening. Then I heard in the background the song 'The Night Chicago Died'. I have had this vision twice.

Source: https://bit.ly/2WZmHsO

Author Jo Ellen Stevens

I saw an earthquake tonight in a vision. A very quick vision: I thought it was the New Madrid Fault. I saw the USA split into two parts.

Source: https://bit.ly/2TIrm07

Shari Straight

Yahweh spoke this to me more than ten years ago and I've been telling all who will listen since then:

"If we divide Israel, God will divide us." What could possibly do that? "An earthquake on the New Madrid fault." I also have been well aware of the significance of the name.

In the past couple years, the Spirit has put a real urgency in me to get on the west side of the Mississippi River.

Source: https://bit.ly/3eon0Dt

Ann Peterson

Then I was shown a short period of relative stillness then I saw the middle of America rise up, then separate into two land masses with a great body of water between the two halves.

Source: https://bit.ly/2ziuTve

Susan Cummings

I enter the vision:

I am standing and underneath my feet, the ground below, begins to sink. It is a sudden violent sinking feeling, like the bottom of the earth is falling or caving in. Everything under your feet sinks while a bright light suddenly flashes all around and a "click" sound in the spirit. This "click" is a dull click sound like a light switch was turned on, and it signaled something, while the flash occurred and exploded in a great light all around us.

Then, this great roar began to slowly grow and increase as the falling ground gave way to a shaking from up and down, to side to side, at the same time. It seemed like the earth is coming apart. The earth violently quakes and breaks up all around. The side to side motion, the up and down, and now forwards and backwards motion.

The land breaks open as it is sinking underneath and quaking in all directions. The middle of the USA breaks open, and splits down the middle, as I stand there, the land masses move.

Source: https://bit.ly/3cLxAmJ

Elane Durham

The area of water in the middle of … the United States was massive, and was widest or most extensive in the north. There were no Great Lakes as I had known them, for all of them had come together into this huge sea that extended northeastward into the ocean. The inland sea also extended southward, filling most of the Mississippi an Missouri River valleys and widening by many, many miles the Mississippi River where it flows into what we know as the Gulf of Mexico. This sea was so vast that I knew it could not be bridged, and so in essence the United States had become as two separate countries.

Source: https://bit.ly/3hofmLG

Chelsie Leigh

So, While living in Costa Rica, my husband had a vision from God. Not a dream. A vision.

Earlier in the night before the vision, he saw a large white being by the foot of our bed. Our baby was staring at the being as well. After I had gone to bed my husband was sitting at the dining table and he said he got a really eerie feeling and the room got really cold. He got up to use the bathroom and when he sat down and looked ahead of him, the wall was gone and instead he saw a map of the United States.

He said there had clearly been a cataclysmic event and that the Mississippi river was enormous and connected to the great lakes. He said the New Madrid had blown out and both the East and West coasts as well as Texas were inundated with water. He was shown "possible areas of survival" and one of them was Colorado. We moved to Colorado because of this..

He was also shown a terrible hurricane prior to being shown the earthquake and the aftermath of the earthquake.

He heard a voice say "If you divide my land, I will divide yours". This vision occurred on Oct. 1st 2016.

Source: https://bit.ly/37l7cPJ

Augusto Perez

It seemed as if the Mississipi River had widened several miles, and now the Great Lakes was connected to the Gulf of Mexico.

Source: https://bit.ly/3herAXe

Lindy Snow Pierce

"Nothing can change it. It is coming. Get ready. My sons and daughters are hearing about this around the world but no one is sounding the alarm due to fear. This nation shall be rocked as never before and shall literally be split in half.* The heavens shall resound with this crack. It shall be heard and felt for miles around. Heaviness is upon the hearts of those I have told. But judgment is coming and it is long past due. I have waited. I've extended My love, but to no avail. A few more will repent before the day but only a handful. They are stubborn and stiff-necked and mock My name. They mock My Son Whose name is holy and not to be defiled. But they use it every day as a curse and drag it through the mud. Their violence and hatred has reached a pinnacle. It is far worse than in the days of Noah. I have stayed My hand because of the intercessors I have there. But no more. The time for judgment has come and I shall let it fall with a thunder. Pray for those who will still repent."

*When He said this I could see the nation split down the Mississippi River. Devastating quakes have hit the river before along the New Madrid Fault and geologists predict they will happen again.

Source: https://bit.ly/2UIgH6q

Amber Dawn

An eagle's eye view of the United States. I saw the United States split in half from a massive earthquake. The madrid fault line. The Lord showed me that this earthquake would cause the great and terrible shaking and that these things would cause the scenarios but that wouldn't be it.

Source: https://bit.ly/2XVE5z5

Rebecca N. Barnes

In the dream I had I was above the USA, I could see all the trees and mountain ranges. I seen a spear come out of the sky, it pierced southern MO and ripped it down all the way to the gulf through Louisiana.

Then I saw it rip up through to the Great Lakes.

I saw st. Louis MO sink under the ground.

It opened in width from st. Louis to hwy 127.

I heard the following exact word's in my spirit "if they divide my land, I will divide their nation."

Source: https://bit.ly/2TIpkNx

Sarah Menet

I saw a huge earthquake in the middle of the United States. It was tremendous and seemed to split the United States in half about where the Mississippi River is. The crack in the earth that resulted was huge and that area totally sank. It was miles wide and it opened up and the earth fell down. It seemed to swallow everything. Then water flowed in from the Gulf of Mexico all the way up to the Great Lakes, only they weren't lakes anymore, they became all part of a big inland sea.

Source: https://bit.ly/2XNNdpJ

Sadhu Sundar Selvaraj

Suddenly I saw an open vision right before my eyes. I saw a mighty angel with a long, drawn sword in his hand. And he stood before me speaking all of these words. Then he said, "This is what will happen to the best friend that will betray Israel and divide Jerusalem."

When he spoke those words, I saw this map of the U.S. like in a three dimensional. It appeared right before my eyes beside the angel. And he took the sword and he pierced right into the heart of the U.S. and he cut it into two. He said, "Likewise will this nation be divided as Jerusalem will be divided." He cut the land into two exactly in the center.

Source: https://bit.ly/3hq4ahE

CHAPTER 6 – WEST COAST SEISMIC EVENTS

The collection of major fault lines that roughly encircles the Pacific Ocean is known as "the Ring of Fire", and it accounts for more than 80 percent of all earthquakes that happen around the globe each year. Of course the entire west coast of the United States and much of the southern coast of Alaska sit directly along the Ring of Fire, but because things have been relatively quiet for the last several decades many of the people that live in these areas have been lulled into a false sense of security.

Unfortunately, it is just a matter of time before that false sense of security is completely shattered.

As you will see below, there will be multiple volcanic eruptions in our western states, a historic earthquake is coming which will radically alter the geography of the entire west coast, and at one point an enormous tsunami will absolutely devastate cities that are located near the Pacific Ocean.

I have been trying to sound the alarm about the seismic activity that is coming to the west coast for years, but unfortunately most of the people living in the region are not interested in such warnings.

Of course I am not the only one that has been issuing ominous warnings. Seismologists have repeatedly told us that the San Andreas fault appears to be "locked and loaded" and that it could potentially "unzip all at once".

If that were to happen, seismologists tell us that the ground level west of the San Andreas fault could suddenly drop by up to 3 feet, and that could potentially result in large portions of southern California suddenly being way below sea level.

In other words, there wouldn't be anything to keep the Pacific Ocean from suddenly rushing in and claiming vast areas along the southern California coastline.

As you read this, you may be thinking that such a thing could never possibly happen, but in recent years scientists have come to the conclusion that such a scenario is actually quite realistic. The following is a direct quote from a major British news source...

The Big One may be overdue to hit California, but scientists near LA have found a new risk for the area during a major earthquake.

They claim that if a major tremor hits the area, it could plunge large parts of California into the sea almost instantly.

The discovery was made after studying the Newport-Inglewood fault, which has long been believed to be one of Southern California's danger zones.

(https://www.dailymail.co.uk/sciencetech/article-4336986/ Ancient-quakes-point-sinking-risk-California-coast.html)

And later on in that same article, there is an absolutely stunning quote from Cal State Fullerton professor Matt Kirby...

Cal State Fullerton professor Matt Kirby, who worked with the Leeper on the study, said the sinking would occur quickly and likely result in part of California being covered by the sea.

"It's something that would happen relatively instantaneously," Prof Kirby said. *"Probably today if it happened, you would see seawater rushing in."*

(https://www.dailymail.co.uk/sciencetech/article-4336986/ Ancient-quakes-point-sinking-risk-California-coast.html)

What this means is that what so many of the prophetic voices have seen has been confirmed by hard science.

We have entered a time when our planet is becoming increasingly unstable, and in recent months we have seen large earthquakes happen all over the globe with frightening regularity.

In Matthew 24, Jesus specifically warned us that earthquakes in diverse places would be one of the signs that His return was drawing near, and so we should definitely expect seismic activity to be increasing if these truly are the last days.

On November 1st, 2019 I had an earthquake dream that really affected me emotionally, and I would like to share that dream with you right now…

I was high up on a hillside, although it was so high that I would be tempted to call it a mountainside. The terrain was very hilly and rocky, and I was with other people inside some sort of structure where we could watch what was happening in the city below.

As I watched, an absolutely enormous earthquake ripped through the houses and buildings in the city. In my dream, I was very emotionally affected by what I was witnessing. I understood that there were people down there that I knew personally. The quake plowed through structures without any resistance at all, and the devastation was immense.

In the dream, I was not given any indication of the location of the earthquake, nor was I given the identities of any of the people that got caught in it. I just knew that there were people that I cared about right in the middle of it.

I have never seen any footage of a quake as powerful as the one that I saw in my dream. Perhaps some Hollywood disaster movies come close to what I saw, but none of those movies ever affected me emotionally like this dream did.

Source: https://bit.ly/2zdgfFK

To me, the terrain in the dream looked like something you would see in the western portion of the United States, but I was never given the location that I was looking at. So I am definitely not claiming that what I saw is for any specific city or geographical location.

It is so important not to add anything and not to subtract anything from the things that God gives to us. He wants us to be faithful to stick to what He has shown us, and going beyond that is a huge error.

With that in mind, there actually have been lots of prophetic voices that have specifically been shown that great natural disasters are going to hit the west coast of the United States. And as you will see, these prophetic voices confirm one another over and over again...

John Paul Jackson

There is a an earthquake that has been predicted to devastate California. Meaning skyscrapers are going to fall that the shape of the United States will change after that earthquake. That won't happen until after there's a storm and major storm is going to come to California. It's either a hurricane of incredible force, or it is a storm of incredible force. But a great, great hurricane, of incredible force is going to come to California, and the earthquake that destroys (California) will not happen until after that takes place. So there's a way of saying, *Okay, I have time*, but that doesn't mean it won't be an earthquake tomorrow 7.5 you know, or next week or two weeks from now of some magnitude. I'm talking to one that changes the shape of California where you don't want to live in California, *anywhere in California*, but that happens or perhaps even the most of the most of the West Coast. Where an inland ocean is formed and and Baja becomes an island and the mouth of the inland ocean forms between between San Diego and Los Angeles.

Source: https://bit.ly/2Utgd3Q

Sadhu Sundar Selvaraj

After the meetings in Costa Mesa, (the next day) we were in Los Angeles airport waiting to board a flight to Houston. While we were waiting, they made an announcement boarding has started. So, we were in the queue waiting to board. At that moment, I heard a voice, "Son of Man, this city is going to be destroyed."

So, I turned around and there was this mighty angel with a big weapon of destruction in his hand. I saw this angel standing beside me and at the same time, I also saw him standing outside the airport. This angel was standing beside me and standing outside near that Encounter restaurant at the same time. This is the same angel. But when he stood outside, he appeared so huge that his head touched the clouds and he had this huge weapon of destruction that looked like a sledgehammer. You know the one that Thor has? Like that.

And he said, "This city will be destroyed by a great earthquake."

When he spoke that, I saw many angels under his leadership and they all stood exactly where the earthquake fault line is going to be in Los Angeles. They all stood in one line with their hammers lifted in their hands, waiting for an order from this captain. Once he gives the order, they will all strike on the ground.

So again, I appealed to this angel, "Why? Why? "

He replied, "Don't you know that these people are worse than Sodom and Gomorrah?"

Source: https://bit.ly/3gZ4bJ5

Michael Boldea

As I fell into a deep sleep I had a dream. I dreamt I was in a hotel room, asleep, when the bed began to shake violently. I knew what was happening right away. Having lived in California in the 1980's I was keenly aware of what an earthquake felt like. Suddenly I was no longer in bed, but high above San Francisco bay, looking down on the golden gate bridge. As I watched it, it began to shudder, break apart, and fall into the waters below. I continued to watch the devastation, seeing buildings collapse, and masses of people trying to find shelter. Then a voice spoke out of the heavens, a voice I had never heard before, a voice of great authority. "I will shake this land from its foundations, such as the eyes of this generation has not seen. The world will stand in awe, and tremble in fear, as even the very geography of this nation will be transformed. My wrath is ready to be poured out, for sin has overrun My temple."

Source: https://bit.ly/2Utgd3Q

Dr. E.R. Lindsey's 1958 Vision

In California, the San Andreas fault will split and the land west of it will sink into the ocean. This will create 150 feet tidal waves which will encircle the world, inundating most coastal cities of the earth. Huge cracks will appear in the ground. Many volcanoes will erupt. The whole earth will shake.

Source: https://bit.ly/2Utgd3Q

Robert Highley

I had this vision last night, I wish I had written down all I had heard and seen but I was too disturbed by it. As I reflected on it this morning I thought I should share what I remember from last night. I was praying for family last night when I saw a vision and heard God's voice. "Do not pray any longer for these disasters to be withheld." A scroll was opened and the United States was written in black and then in blood red next to it was the word judgement written thickly in what appeared to be blood. I saw the earth like a globe and then it panned to the West Coast of the United States. A huge fiery explosion went off in the Pacific Northwest near the coast and then I saw California begin to flood. The view panned high above the earth and I saw that the state of California was covered far inland by a giant Tsunami.

Source: https://bit.ly/2XUg6z1

Dr. Melanie Rettler

It was like I was dropped into a situation and hovering just a couple feet off the ground I knew I was in California and I was facing east.

There were dead bodies all around and injured people. Something catastrophic just occurred. I heard people saying and screaming, get to the hills, get to the hills, and they were running eastward.

There was a crack in the ground in front of me and I knew that it was too late for all those people, only the people already at or on the hills had any chance. I knew that the hills that they were talking about where east of were I had been. The whole vision seem to last only a few seconds.

Source: https://bit.ly/2Utgd3Q

John Paul Jackson

Volcanoes are going to erupt in the Northwestern part of the United States. Cities will be dramatically impacted. There will be things that happen that are just unheard of.

Source: https://bit.ly/2YnVRKo

Dr. Maurice Sklar

I saw a massive earthquake that just seemed to crack off the coast of California. It reminded me of a Saltine cracker that just cracked in two! The great cities along the West coast just fell into the ocean, all the way from Mexico up to Alaska and giant waves flooded inland until much of the West Coast just wasn't there! It had disappeared into the Pacific Ocean.

Source: https://bit.ly/2Utgd3Q

Wendy Alec

And I saw a mighty shaking and trembling begin under the earth. And the Lord said, "From under the Pacific it shall come, in fire and in water it shall come."

It was hardly noticeable at first but it was as though the whole city froze as one and then the shaking and the terror and then the fire came. I saw a horrifying inferno, a literal inferno.

I saw ravaged land and ravaged cities. But one city received the full force of this terror and earthquake and this is what the warning was crying out "THE BAY, THE BAY."

And I saw the heavens were black, blacker than black and there was no light – all light was extinguished.

And the smoke continued to rise and thousands upon thousands of this city were killed at the first strike, but I saw a second strike.

In the second strike I saw water devastating parts of the west coast, to the north, beware the north, the northern California coastline.

I still saw plumes of smoke rising from charred buildings. There was not just one city affected. It was more than one on the northern California coast. People were bleeding and dying.

Source: https://bit.ly/3dbyJ83

Missionary Patti Rowe's 1974 Vision

I saw a big bridge crumble and fall into the water below. Northern California came to my mind. The bridge didn't just fall, it crumbled into small pieces. It happened suddenly.

Source: https://bit.ly/2YtCyzA

Nita Johnson

Starting with the West Coast, the voice would speak and that same silvery light would shoot down from the direction of heaven like a laser beam onto the map. The light would follow the path directed by the voice and then effects would follow as I will explain. First, the voice cried out-'The West Coast, California, Oregon and Washington, starting from the southern most tip all the way up to Seattle, will suffer natural disasters, such as earthquakes, floods and fire, and enemy attack. "The line shot up the map taking most of California and leaving only a small section that bordered on Arizona and Nevada. It went up through Oregon taking about half of that state and then on up through Washington, taking about one-third of that state, then out toward the ocean through Seattle. The minute the line touched Seattle, everything west of the line disappeared.

Source: https://bit.ly/2BdcvEF

Elane Durham

Earthquakes had occurred and there had been hurricanes and fierce storms — the whole country had been ravaged by these things. I could also see massive fires burning here and there — not so much the flames as the smoke that was ascending toward me — as huge areas of the country seemed to be burning or burned. There were also explosions in some areas, sort of like sheet lightning in a dark sky, that were doing great damage.

Where Washington and Oregon had been there were mostly islands, the water coming inland over most of California and Arizona and parts of Utah and Nevada. Yet there were also islands there, massive ones, so it wasn't like it was all ocean...

Source: https://bit.ly/2Utgd3Q

Perry Stone

Early this morning I saw another detailed tsunami dream that was so vivid and detailed that it disturbed me greatly. On the West Coast, a major split occurred in the ocean causing the Pacific's waves to rise high in all directions. I saw dangerous waves coming in the distance and yelled, "Get to the mountains!"

As we began rushing to a high place I could see the waves hit the coasts and rush violently into the streets of cities. The scene shifted and I found myself in a house on a high mountain. The people were quite wealthy and there were reports on the news of the horrific damage and destruction. I can still see the waves in my minds eye.

Source: https://bit.ly/3eOwS6z

Michelle Walcott

While I was driving down Coast Hwy towards Yaquina Bay bridge, I was at a red light. All of a sudden I saw a huge wall of water to my right and it must have been 100 feet or more tall. It happened so suddenly that I ducked and then realized it was a Vision of a Tsunami.

I sat there shaken for what seemed to be a long while and I hear a voice tell me that there would be a Tsunami hit the West Coast and it would be so large that it would move inland for several miles. I am not sure how far it would go. I just know it was told it would be huge.

Source: https://bit.ly/2X0InET

Rebecca Cooper

"I Was Raised Over the City of Portland, Oregon and as I Looked the Floodgates Opened Up and Thousands of Dead Bodies Were Tumbling Over Each Other Inside and Outside the City, as I Looked out in Horror, I Could See the Massive Water (Tsunami) and Again Unexplainable and Unimaginable Horror!"

Source: https://bit.ly/2ZQnv52

Sarah Menet

I saw a huge earthquake strike Utah and then California. There were earthquakes all over California, but were especially devastating in the Los Angeles and San Francisco areas.

These earthquakes triggered volcanoes all over the West. They started spewing a tremendous amount of ash and smoke into the air and the air became very dark and dirty. The sun was darkened even more because of the smoke and the ash that started raining down everywhere.

I also saw huge waves of water sweep over the West Coast and then I realized that it was happening all over the coastal cities of the entire world. Los Angeles was almost swept completely away. The waves were huge.

Source: https://bit.ly/2XNNdpJ

Steve Pursell

In recent months several times, and again last night, I have received visions of a huge tsunami coming into the San Francisco Bay in California. I have seen two different scenes, both of which are of the tsunami engulfing a different bridge. The two bridges I saw engulfed are the Carquinez Bridge and the Martinez Bridge, both of which are back deeper in the bay waters than the Golden Gate and the Bay Bridge, the latter two being closer out towards the Pacific Ocean. In the one vision the tsunami was tall enough to completely engulf the entire bridge all the way over the top of the Martinez Bridge which is 138 feet high. And, since the Carquinez Bridge is 394 feet tall, it may be close 300 feet tall.

Source: https://bit.ly/3f3V6gc

Sean Harper

I found myself in my car driving through Montana. My friends who lived in California at the time spoke to me, "Thank God we got out of California when we did! There is nothing left of it!" At this I sat confused. I asked, "what happened!?" They responded, "A great Earthquake shook the state to the ground! How do you not know?"

The third person in the car said, "I'm glad my father told me prepare, but now I have nothing to eat because I did not prepare enough!"

Source: https://bit.ly/2BIvs2o

Sister Hyang Mi Moon

But in within that moment, my body flew up into the air and I was above California.

In front of my eyes, I was witnessing the scene of a horrific earthquake and tsunami. The calamity was overwhelming the state of California (But I am not sure if the initial earthquake is going to shake the whole state or parts of it). The scene included cliffs on the shore crumbling with buildings and trees being engulfed by water.

A great and fearful event was occurring right in front of my eyes. My flesh, soul, and spirit were shouting with one voice. "Noooo-oooo!!! Nooooooooooooo!!!!" What was being shown to me was too great to bear. I could not do anything but scream. My whole being was screaming. As I screamed, my body and soul trembled in fear.

I saw people dying. They were dying in vain. I saw the empty stares of the people. They did not have time to scream. They died as they were swallowed by the tsunami. Some attempted to escape by car. Some were running to escape. I saw the horrible fearful expression on their faces and eyes. It was a melting pot of terror and pandemonium.

Source: https://bit.ly/2CjBbvE

Dan Carlson

At this point, Los Angeles came into clear focus. Our vantage point had shifted so that we appeared to be much closer to the city. Its tall buildings and landmarks were now easily discernible. In fact, I was amazed at how smog-free the atmosphere was that day.

By now, a huge crack had opened up through the heart of the city and the sections on either side were tilting sharply, first one way and then another.

The force of the movement was so violent, and the angle of tilt so steep, that the tallest buildings, first on the left and then on the right, were literally thrust to the ground with angry violence.

I was amazed at the suddenness of their collapse. I suppose I had expected them to topple over gradually, like a falling tree. But, no, they came crashing down as though they had been kicked over by a giant boot. The entire area caved in, sinking quickly into the open split.

Within minutes, the once proud city was a sea of churning water. No sign of it remained—not a building, tower, road or bridge. All of it was now on the bottom of the sea.

The scene now changed and we found ourselves on a distant hilltop, sitting in a restaurant outside porch and looking with bewilderment at the vastness of the Pacific Ocean; knowing—

MICHAEL SNYDER

but hardly believing—that beneath its rhythmic waves were the debris and remains of the once-famous and proud city of Los Angeles.

The prophecies had been fulfilled. So few had accepted them. Signs had been given, but the majority—pagans and Christians alike—had scoffed at them.

Source: https://bit.ly/2yDgjy3

Lastly, I would like to share Joe Brandt's entire vision from 1937 with you. Please note that many of the specific details that he witnessed during this supernatural experience did not exist in 1937, but they perfectly describe our current time…

Joe Brandt's 1937 Vision Of The Coming Earthquake

THE DAY OF THE EARTHQUAKE

I woke up in the hospital room with a terrific headache- as if the whole world was revolving inside my brain. I remember, vaguely, the fall from my horse-Blackie. As I lay there, pictures began to form in my mind-pictures that moved with the speed of lightning-pictures that revolved-pictures that stood still. I seemed to be in another world. Whether it was the future, or whether it was some ancient land, I could not say.

Then slowly, like the silver screen of the "talkies", but with colour and smell and sound, I seemed to find myself in Los Angeles. It was Los Angeles-it was bigger, much bigger, and buses and odd shaped cars crowded the city streets. I thought about Hollywood Boulevard, and I found myself, there, on Hollywood Boulvard. Whether this is true, I don't know, but there were a lot of guys about my age with beards and wearing, some of them, earrings. All the girls wore real short skirts… and they slouched along, moving like a dance. I wondered if I could talk to them,

86

and I said "hello", but they didn't hear or see me. I decided that I would look as funny to them as they looked to me. I tried, for awhile, that crazy kind of walk. I guess it is something you have to learn. I couldn't to it. I noticed there was a quietness about the air, a kind of stillness. Something else was missing, something that should be there.

At first, I couldn't figure it out, I didn't know what it was-then I did. THERE WERE NO BIRDS. I listened. I walked two blocks north on the Blvd...All houses...no birds. I wondered what had happened to them. Had they gone away? Where? Again, I could hear the stillness. I had never experienced anything like it. I listened...just the stillness.

Then, I knew something was going to happen. I wondered what year it was. It certainly was not 1937. I saw a newspaper on the corner with a picture of the president. It surely wasn't Mr. Roosevelt. He was bigger, heavier, big ears. If it wasn't 1937, I wondered what year it was. It looked like 1969...but I wasn't sure. My eyes weren't working just right..

Someone was coming...someone in 1937... it was that fat nurse ready to take my temperature. I woke up. Crazy dream (There are pages here about a similar dream occurring-finding himself in Los Angeles-although it was the next day (in 1937) it was the same day in Los Angeles, and the dream would continue where the last dream left off.) My headache is worse. It is a wonder I didn't get killed on that horse. I've had another crazy dream, back in Hollywood. Those people. Why do they dress like that I wonder? I found myself back on the Boulevard. I was waiting for something to happen. Something BIG was going to happen and I was going to be there. I looked up at the clock down by that big theatre. It was 10 minutes to 4. Something BIG was going to happen. I walked down the street. In the concrete in front of a theatre they had names of stars. I recognized a few of them. The other names I had never heard. I was getting bored. I wanted to get back to the hospital in Fresno, and I wanted to stay there on the Boulevard., even if nobody could see me. Those crazy kids. Why are they dressed like that? Maybe it is some big Halloween doings, but it don't seem like Halloween. More like early spring.

There was that sound again. that LACK OF SOUND. STILLNESS, STILLNESS, STILLNESS. Don't these people KNOW that the birds have gone somewhere? The QUIET IS GETTING BIGGER AND BIGGER. I KNOW IT IS GOING TO HAPPEN. SOMETHING IS GOING TO HAPPEN. Something is happening now!

It sure did. She woke me up, grinning and smiling, that fat nurse again. "It's time for your milk, kiddo," she says. Gosh, old woman of 30 acting like the cat's pyjamas. Next time maybe she'll bring hot chocolate.

THE MOMENT OF THE HAPPENING

Where have I been. Where haven't I been! I've been to the ends of the earth and back. I've been to the end of the world. There isn't anything left. Not even Fresno, even though I'm lying here right this minute. If only my eyes would get a little clearer so I can write all this down. Nobody will believe me, anyway.

I'm going back to that last moment on the Boulevard. Some sweet kid went past, dragging a little boy (twins, I guess) by each hand. Her skirt was up–well, pretty high–and she had a tired look. I thought for a minute I could ask her about the birds, what had happened to them, and then, I remembered she didn't see me. Her hair was all frowzy, way out all over her head. A lot of them looked like that, but she looked so tired and like she was sorry about something. I guess she was sorry BEFORE it happened, because it surely did happen.

There was a funny smell. I don't like it. A smell like sulphur, sulphuric acid, a smell like death. For a minute, I thought I was back in chem. (chemistry). When I looked around for the girl, she was gone. I wanted to find her for some reason. It was if I knew something was going to happen and I could stay with her, help her. She was gone, and I walked half a block, then saw the clock again. My eyes seemed glued on that clock. I couldn't move. I just waited. It was FIVE MINUTES TO FOUR O'CLOCK ON A SUNNY AFTERNOON. I thought I would stand there looking at that clock forever waiting for the something to come.

Then, when it came, it was nothing. It was just nothing. It wasn't nearly as hard as the earthquake we had two years ago. The ground shook, just an instant. People looked at each other, surprised. Then they laughed, I laughed too. So this was what I had been waiting for. This funny little shake. It meant nothing. I was relieved and I was disappointed. What had I been waiting for? I started back up the Boulevard, moving my legs like those kids. How do they do it?

I never found out. I felt as if the ground wasn't solid under me. I knew I was dreaming and yet I wasn't dreaming. There was that smell again–coming like from the ocean. I was getting to the 5 and 10 (Newberry's?) and I saw the look on the kids' faces. Two of them were right in front of me, coming my way. Both with beards. One with earrings. One said: "let's get out of this place. Let's go back East." He seemed scared. It was as if the sidewalks were trembling – but you couldn't seem to see them. Not with your eyes you couldn't. An old lady had a dog, a little white dog, and she stopped and looked scared, and grabbed him in her arms and said," Let's go home, Frou, Frou. Mamma is going to take you home." That poor old lady, hanging on to her dog. I got scared. Real scared.

I remembered the girl. She was way down the block, probably. I started to run. I ran and ran, and the ground kept trembling. But I couldn't see it. I couldn't feel it. But I knew it was trembling. Everybody looked scared. They looked terrible. One young lady just sit down on the sidewalk all doubled up. She kept saying "earthquake, it's THE earthquake." over and over. But I COULDN"T SEE THAT ANYTHING WAS DIFFERENT.

Then, when it came. How it came. Like nothing in God's world. Like nothing. It was the scream of a siren, long and low, or the scream of a woman I heard having a baby when I was a kid. It was awful. It was as if something- some monster- was PUSHING UP THE SIDEWALKS. You felt it long before you saw it, as if the sidewalks wouldn't hold anymore. I looked out at the cars. They were honking but not scared. They just kept moving. They didn't seem to know yet that anything was happening. Then, that white car, that baby half-sized one, came sprawling from the inside lane right against the curb. The girl who was driving just sat there. She sat there with her eyes staring, as if she couldn't move, but I could hear her. She whimpered. Like a little girl. She made funny noises. I watched her, thinking of the other girl.

I said that it was a dream and I would wake up. But I didn't wake up. The shaking had started again, but this time different. It was a nice shaking, like a cradle being rocked for a minute, and then I saw the middle of the Boulevard. seemed to be breaking in two. The concrete looked as if it were being pushed straight up by some giant shovel. It was breaking in two. That is why the girl's car went out of control.. AND THEN A LOUD SOUND AGAIN, LIKE I'VE NEVER HEARD BEFORE...THEN HUNDREDS OF SOUNDS...ALL KINDS OF SOUNDS... children, and women and those crazy guys with earrings. They were all moving, it seemed, some of them above the sidewalk. I can't describe it. They were LIFTED UP. and the waters kept oozing...oozing. The cries. It was awful. I woke up. I never want to have that dream again.

THE EARTHQUAKE

It came again. Like the first time which was a preview and all I could remember was that it was the end of the world. I was right back there–all that crying. Right in the middle of it. My eardrums felt as if they were going to burst. Noise everywhere. People falling down, some of them bad hurt. Pieces of buildings, chips, flying in the air. One hit me hard on the side of the face, but I didn't seem to feel it.

I wanted only to wake up, to get away from this place. It had been fun in the beginning, the first dream, when I kind of knew I was going to dream the end of the world or something. This was terrible. There were older people in the cars. Most of the kids were in the street. But those old guys were yelling bloody murder, as if anybody could help them.. Nobody could help them. Nobody could help them.

It was then that I felt myself lifted up. Maybe I had died. I don't know. But I was over the city. It was tilting toward the ocean-like tilting a picnic table. The buildings were holding, better than you could believe. They were holding. They were holding. The people saw they were holding and they tried to cling to them or get inside. It was fantastic. Like a building had a will of its own. Everything else breaking around them, and they were holding, holding. I was up over them-looking down. I started to root for them. Hold that line, I said. Hold that line. Hold that line. I wanted to cheer, to shout, to scream. If the buildings held, those buildings on the Boulevard., maybe the girl-the girl with the two kids-maybe she could get inside.

It looked that way for a long time, maybe three minutes, and three minutes was like forever. Everybody was trying to get inside. They were going to hold. You knew they were going to hold, even if the waters kept coming up. Only they didn't. I've never imagined what it would be like for a building to die. A building dies just like a person. It gives way, some of the bigger ones did just that. They began to crumble, like an old man with palsy, who couldn't take it anymore. They crumble right down to nothing. And the little ones screamed like mad-over and above the roar of the people. They were mad about dying. But buildings die. I couldn't look anymore at the people. I kept wanting to get higher. I kept willing myself to go higher.

Then I seemed to be out of it all, but I could see. I seemed to be up on Big Bear near San Bernardino, but the funny thing is that I could see everywhere. I knew what was happening. The earth seemed to start to tremble again. I could feel it even though I was up high. This time it lasted maybe twelve seconds, and it was gentle. You couldn't believe anything so gentle could cause so much damage. But then I saw the streets of Los Angeles-and everything between the San Bernardino mountains and L.A. It was all tilting toward the ocean, houses, everything that was left. I could see the big lanes-dozens of big lanes still loaded with cars-five lanes in one place, and all the cars sliding the same way.

Now the ocean was coming in, moving like a huge snake across the land. I wondered how long it was, and I could see the clock, even though I wasn't there on the Boulevard. It was 4:29. It had been half an hour. I was glad I couldn't hear the crying any more. But I could see everything. I could see everything.

THE OTHER CITIES

Then, like looking at a huge map of the world, I could see what was happening on the land and with people. San Francisco was feeling it, but she was not in any way like Hollywood or Los Angeles. I seemed to see it was the GARLOCK FAULT, not just the SAN ANDREAS that was rocking San Francisco. It was moving just like that earthquake movie with Jeanette McDonald and Gable. I could see all those mountains coming together-the Sierra Nevada, and the San Andreas and Garlock.

I knew what was going to happen to San Francisco-it was going to turn over, because of Garlock. It would turn upside down. It went quickly, because of the twisting, I guess. It seemed much faster than Hollywood, but then I wasn't exactly there. I was a long, long way off.

I shut my eyes for a long time-I guess ten minutes-and when I opened them I saw Grand Canyon, that great big gap was closing in, and Boulder Dam was being pushed from underneath. And then, Nevada, and on up to Reno. Way down south, way down Baja, California, Mexico too. It looked like some volcano down there was erupting, along with everything else.

I saw the map of South America, especially Colombia. Another volcano-eruption-shaking violently. Venezuela seemed to be having some king of volcanic activity. Away off in the distance, I could see Japan, on a Fault, too. It was so far off-not easy to see, because I was still on Big Bear Mountain, but Japan started to go into the sea. I couldn't tell time, then, and the people looked like dolls, far away. I couldn't hear the screaming, but I could see the surprised look on their faces. They looked so surprised.. They were all like dolls. It was so far away I could hardly see it. In a minute or two it seemed over. Everybody was gone. There was nobody left.

I didn't know time now. I couldn't see a clock. I tried to see the island of Hawaii. I could just see huge tidal waves...beating against it. The people on the streets were getting wet, and they were scared. But I didn't see anybody going into the sea. I seemed way around the globe. More flooding. Is the world going to be drenched? Constantinople. Black Sea rising. Suez Canal, for some reason seemed to be drying up. SICILY.. she doesn't hold. I could see map. Mt Etna is shacking. A lot of this area seemed to go, but it seemed to be earlier or later.

I wasn't sure of time, now. ENGLAND.....huge floods-but no tidal waves. Water, water everywhere, but no one going into the sea. People were frightened and crying. Some places they fell in the streets on their knees and started to pray for the world. I didn't know the English were emotional. Ireland, Scotland-all kinds of churches were crowded-it seemed night and day. People were carrying candles and everybody was crying for California, Nevada, parts of Colorado- maybe all of it, even Utah.

Everybody was crying-most of them didn't even know anybody in California, Nevada, Utah, but they were crying as if they were blood kin. Like one family. Like it happened to them. NEW YORK was coming into view-she was still there, nothing had happened, yet water level was way up. Here, things were different. People were running in the streets yelling-"end of world". Kids ran into restaurants and ate everything in sight. I saw a shoe store with all the shoes gone in about five minutes. Fifth Avenue- everybody running. Some radio blasting from a loud speaker that in a few minutes, power might be shut off. They must control themselves. Five girls were running like mad toward the Y.W.C.A., that place on Lexington or somewhere. They ran like they were scared to death. BUT NOTHING WAS HAPPENING IN NEW YORK. I saw an old lady with garbage cans, filling them with water. Everybody seemed scared to death. Some people looked dazed. The streets seemed filled with loud speakers. It wasn't daylight. It was night. I saw, like the next day, and everything was topsy turvy. Loud speakers again about fuel tanks broken in areas-shortage of oil. People seemed to be looting markets.

Oregon, Washington, The Dakotas, Missouri, Minnesota, Canada

I saw a lot of places that seemed safe, and people were not scared. Especially the rural areas. Here everything was almost as if nothing had happened. People seemed headed to these places, some on foot, some in cars (that still had fuel). I heard – or somehow I knew – that somewhere in the Atlantic land had come up. A lot of land. I was getting awful tired. I wanted to wake up I wanted to go back to the girl-to know where she was-she and those two kids. I found myself back in Hollywood-and it was still 4:29. I wasn't up on Big Bear then- I was perched over Hollywood. I was just there. It seemed perfectly natural in my dream.

T.V., Radio, Ham Operators

I could hear now. I could hear, someplace, a radio station blasting out-telling people not to panic. They were dying in the streets. There were picture stations with movies-some right in Hollywood-these were carrying on, with all the shaking. One fellow (in the picture (TV) station) was a little short guy who should have been scared to death. But he wasn't. He kept shouting and reading instructions. Something about helicopters or planes would go over-some kind of planes-but I knew they couldn't.

Things were happening in the atmosphere. The waves were rushing up now. Waves. Such waves. Nightmare waves. Then, I saw again, Boulder Dam, going down...pushing together, pushing together breaking apart-No, Grand Canyon was pushing together, and Boulder Dam was breaking apart. It was still daylight. All these radio stations went off at the same time-Boulder Dam had broken. I wondered how everybody would know about it-people back East. That was when I saw the "ham radio operators". I saw them in the oddest places, as if I were right there with them. Like the little guy with glasses. They kept sounding the alarm. One kept saying: "This is California. We are going into the sea. This is California. We are going into the sea.. Get to the high places. Get to the mountains. All states west-this is California. We are going to the – We are going to the" – I thought he was going to say" sea". But I could see him. He was inland, but the waters had come in. His hand was still clinging to the table, he was trying to get up, so that once again he could say: "This is California we are going into the sea. This is California we are going into the sea." I seemed to hear this, over and over, for what seemed hours-just those words.

They kept it up until the last minute-all of them-calling out "Get to the Mountains-This is California.-We are going into the sea." I woke up. It didn't seem as if I had been dreaming. I have never been so tired. For a minute or two, I thought it had happened. I wondered about two things. I hadn't seen all what happened to Fresno (his home) and I hadn't found out what happened to that girl. I've been thinking about it all morning. I'm going home tomorrow. It was just a dream. It was nothing more.

Nobody in the future on Hollywood Boulevard. is going to be wearing earrings-and those beards. Nothing like that is ever going to happen. That girl was so real to me-that girl with those two kids. It won't ever happen-but if it did, how could I tell her (maybe she isn't even born yet) to move away from California when she has her twins-and she can't be on the Boulevard. that day. She was so real!

The other thing-those ham operators-hanging on like that-over and over-saying the same thing: "This is California. We are going into the sea. This is California. We are going into the sea. Get to the mountains. Get to the hilltops. California, Nevada Colorado, Arizona, Utah. This is California. We are going into the sea." I guess I'll hear that for days.

Source: https://bit.ly/2Utgd3Q

CHAPTER 7 – EAST COAST TSUNAMI

Someday, a giant tsunami that is hundreds of feet high will slam into the east coast of the United States. This unprecedented disaster will wipe out dozens of major cities and instantly kill millions of people. In recent years, God has sent warning after warning about this catastrophic event, and in this chapter I will share many examples of those warnings.

Some of those that have been shown that an east coast tsunami is coming have also been shown that it will be caused by a large asteroid striking the Atlantic Ocean. And in some cases, people have seen that the asteroid breaks into multiple pieces and that there are multiple impact locations in the Atlantic.

But before we get to what prophetic voices have specifically been shown over the last several decades, I want to share an ancient prophecy from the 1100s that was given by a German Christian known as St. Hildegard. It appears that she also saw that an enormous celestial object will hit the Atlantic Ocean and that this will cause a massive tsunami to hit coastal cities...

Before the Comet comes, many nations, the good excepted, will be scoured with want and famine. The great nation in the ocean that is inhabited by people of different tribes and descent by an earthquake, storm and tidal waves will be devastated. It will be divided, and in great part submerged. That nation will also have many misfortunes at sea, and lose its colonies in the east through a Tiger and a Lion. The Comet by its tremendous pressure, will force much out of the ocean and flood many countries, causing much want and many plagues. All coastal cities will be fearful and many of them will be destroyed by tidal waves, and most living creatures will be killed and even those who escape will die from a horrible disease. For in none of these cities does a person live according to the laws of God.

Source: https://bit.ly/2UFv5fv

When St. Hildegard was alive, the United States did not even exist yet. But to me, the "great nation in the ocean that is inhabited by people of different tribes and descent" certainly sounds like a perfect description of the United States. And as we have already covered in this book, America will be physically "divided" by a huge earthquake along the New Madrid fault.

Could it be possible that more than 800 years ago she was shown the exact same things that so many prophetic voices are seeing today?

Sadly, most Americans have never even heard about these warnings, and they have absolutely no idea that someday a disaster of this nature will suddenly strike our nation.

Of course the Bible also contains a prophecy about a celestial object hitting the ocean. In Revelation chapter 8, the Apostle John was shown that "a great mountain burning with fire was cast into the sea", and this absolutely enormous object causes immense death and destruction.

Did the Apostle John see the same event that so many others in our day and time are also being shown?

Please keep that question in mind as you read through the following prophecies...

Evangelist Joan Schmitz

It was then that I saw something that looked like a giant wall standing off the shores of New York City. As I watched the giant wave, I pondered what it was. Then the Lord opened my understanding, and I was made to know that it was a tidal wave. As I watched the giant wave, it began to fold over and go over the skyscrapers. It was then that I cried out to the Lord saying, "Lord, your people, your people!" He then replied, "The peoples of the earth shall be brought together upon one common ground — SURVIVAL!"

Source: https://bit.ly/3h0nGRJ

Dr. Roxanne Brant's 1973 Vision

Late one afternoon in early September I was relaxing after a hard day's work, thinking about business details, when the Holy Spirit came upon me and opened my eyes to see what was to come in these next few years. First, I saw a very clear picture of Florida. The southern two-thirds of the state was baked dry in the sun and in a state of severe drought. But I saw clouds filled with rain move down and gently drop their moisture over the northeast corner of Florida, exactly in the location where I had bought the land. Then, I sensed that something awesome was about to happen to the southern half of Florida, and as I shifted my gaze southward, the most eerie and incredible thing I have ever witnessed then occurred. The ocean, like a giant monster rose silently and calmly and began to move across the land. It moved miles inland, flooding everything in its path.

Source: https://bit.ly/37s7Vyh

Dr. Maurice Sklar

I saw a flood, like the ocean, like the tsunami in Japan, except it was BIGGER. It swept over a good portion of south east....Florida particularly. I don't know what caused it, but I saw a big giant wave just cover a portion of the south east under water. I saw the same thing from the middle of America. It was three different places that I saw this flooding, this water. It made parts of America just go under the ocean. You couldn't see it anymore. Also into Canada a little bit. I didn't see Canada for some reason. I think this dream was focused on America.

Source: https://bit.ly/2TCTEta

Augusto Perez

Slowly, as I continued to look I was able to understand what was being written in the skies. I began to read about future events that were going to take place right before the return of the LORD Jesus Christ. Then, I began to see what was being written in the skies, as if a movie was being played right in front of me. Then suddenly without warning, I was sucked right into the vision that was being shown to me. What I saw, was beyond anything that I have ever thought possible. Big chunks of America began disappearing from the map. I was up in the sky and I saw three quarters of Florida covered with water, except for the northern part.

Source: https://bit.ly/30qtuOl

Shari Straight

In 1998, Yah took me up again into the upper atmosphere over Florida and I saw what looked like from about Orlando and south completely under water. There was no land mass sticking up above the ocean. It was like a straight line drawn from west to east. The land north of what I thought was Olrando was above water and all that below what I thought was Orlando was gone, submerged. When I told a couple friends what I'd seen, they told me of dreams they'd had of a tsunami washing over the state. As they described it, I could see it with the eye of my spirit and I knew that I had seen the aftermath. It was so real to me too.

Source: https://bit.ly/3eon0Dt

Dr. Patricia Green

When I was lifted up, I could see that the wave was like hundreds of feet tall. It wasn't just a little wave. It was hundreds of feet tall. Jesus spoke these words to me. He said,

"This wave will hit the east coast." He said, "Warn the people to get out. This mighty wave will devastate coastal cities and wash inland for many miles. Florida will be decimated. Washington D.C. will be under water. New York Harbor will flood the city. In North Carolina, the water will come as far as the mountains. The water will not go beyond the Appalachian mountains."

He said,

"There are those that will not believe what you are reporting. They will perish in the wave." He said, "Millions of people will lose their lives." He said, "Nothing of this magnitude happens on the earth unless I speak it through my prophets. I have shown many of my prophets this tsunami, and they are also reporting it will happen."

Source: https://bit.ly/36KAbfa

Ann Peterson

Here is the account of the vision dealing with the comets and the destruction to befall America that I was given.

In April 2001 I was moved to ask God what was coming at us.

The question was as generic as that...but not the answer.

I was then shown North America on a globe. I saw three balls of fire streaking across the globe. One hits in the Gulf of Mexico... another hits near the east coast of Florida...and the third is further out in the Atlantic.

I then see America get smaller. Florida is washed over as well as much of the east coast and the coastal areas of the Gulf. I asked if people would be warned of this event in any way. I was told that this was the warning. I asked again about the others that did not hear or see initial warnings. I heard that there would be a very small window of opportunity for people to get out of harms way...but most would still not listen. Then the only "close-up" view I got was of I-95...it was a death trap...and those were the words I heard too.

Source: https://bit.ly/2ziuTve

Susan Rhodes

In May 2016, I had the vision of Tsunami hitting the East Coast. I saw nearly all of FL underwater. This sister is right, that there will be no warning, much of the Eastern Seaboard will be gone too. NYC will be destroyed, NJ and RI underwater as will much of the coast line will be underwater. No food will come by ship because the ports will be gone. Gulf Coast States will also lose ground to the water surge. It will cause water to flow up the Mississippi River and an Earthquake will divide it causing the country to be divided by two parts. The bridges will fall into the River. Other rivers that connect to it will also be affected.

Source: https://bit.ly/2AkqYP8

John W. Johnston

Fall of 2005 -I went into a deep sleep and had a dream I was on the boardwalk in Virginia Beach. It was night time and I think it was about 2:00 am. I put my foot up on the railing and was looking out over the ocean. There was what looked like a full moon on the horizon. I noticed just underneath the moon was a giant black wall on the horizon. The moon was reflecting white caps off the wall. As I stood there looking out into the Atlantic Ocean I realized that the white caps are from a massive tidal wave heading to shore. It was about 300 foot high. I felt the realization that it was too late to warn the people and the dream ended.In the fall of the following year, 2006 I had the same dream again.In January 2008, I had the same dream except this time I started running to peoples houses to wake them up and warn them, but it was too late.I feel like this tidal wave is a real tidal wave that is going to hit the eastern seaboard. I also believe this tidal wave might represent in the spiritual, a tidal wave of satanic destruction that is coming to destroy the people.To my amazement, in the months of April, May and June of this year (2008), I saw a group of people on the boardwalk in Virginia Beach anointing the railings and banisters with anointing oil. Even though I knew why they were doing this, I pretended like I was just curious and asked them. They told me they were anointing the banisters and railings for the whole Virginia Beach boardwalk because they had dreams that Virginia Beach was going to be hit with a giant tidal wave.

Source: https://bit.ly/2WZmHsO

Augusto Perez

I was in the beach coast (I think it was the East Coast, but I am not sure) staying on the 3rd floor hotel, when I saw looking down on the beach the water beginning to retreat rapidly into the sea and the seashore becoming dry. I knew instantly it was a tsunami coming. I went down and tried to warn the people telling them they had twenty minutes to get out, but no one believed me. They kept on having a good time in the beach. In the distance I could see people in boats. I went back up to my room, and suddenly I saw boats of all sizes, catamarans and colorful sailboats by the hundreds coming in. People were scared and jumping off their boats as they ran towards the shore with a look of panic and horror in their faces as I could start to see the giant tsunami in the distance making its way towards the beach.

Source: https://bit.ly/2WZmHsO

Javonna Williamson-Peng

I was in the mountains of North Carolina in a house looking out the back window of the house toward the mountain top I seen the figure of the Lord standing there! He called my name to come stand with him and I was excited to do just that! As I stood next to him he asked to show me something and I said of course Lord I want to see.. so he told me to look toward Florida and then within quickly flashing seconds I seen every major highway through Florida jammed packed with cars, people trying to flee for their life, people running and screaming.. then I looked toward the east coast waters off Florida coast and I seen an asteroid impact the waters between Florida and the Puerto Rican islands. Smaller meteor fragments also impacted the west coast of Florida waters.. the impact from both sides caused 1,000 ft tsunami waves to come barreling toward Florida .. then in one more flash I seen the tsunami waves close in on the entire state.. the whole state of Florida was gone!! I woke up crying and shaking.. upon waking up and praying after, the Holy Spirit prompted me to read Revelation chapter 6 and 7. I believe the asteroid represents the third trumpet judgment.. where it speaks of a mountain being thrown into the sea..

Source: https://bit.ly/36FB494

Melisa Peggs

God than showed me a VERY LARGE tsunami wave coming into NYC. It literally covered all of NYC. God than took me underwater and showed me NYC.

I than had a conversation with God and asked Him why the people of NYC didn't listen. He said they loved their riches and their life more than they loved Him.

Source: https://bit.ly/2XdIBss

Akida Lavender

I keep having these dreams about a terrible surge of water hitting The East Coast. One city I seen devastated was definitely New York City. The water rose above the tallest buildings. In my dream the water came storming in too fast for anyone to escape it.

Source: https://bit.ly/2X7HLh3

Ron Putnam

In my latest dream, I was in a hotel with lots of windows that could see NYC from a distance. It seemed like about 10 or 20 miles away, but I could see everything in the dream, as if it was closer (please know, I have never been to NYC, except the airport passing to another location).

In the dream, as I was looking out the window, I saw a huge tsunami coming over the tops of the largest buildings and the statue of liberty knocking over and the water rushing my direction.

Source: https://bit.ly/3cR4Zwk

Brad Hay

I dreamt that a massive tidal wave was coming in from the Gulf of Mexico and moving from the southeast towards the northwest. It looked to be at least 100' high as it covered the trees and buildings. They tidal wave had made it to central Louisiana (around Lafayette) and was still moving across the State with a lot of force. The only event I think that could cause that large of a tidal wave that could reach that far inland is a comet or asteroid impact in the Atlantic or Gulf of Mexico.

Source: https://bit.ly/2M8xVFn

Lygia Maria

I saw the Atlantic Coast of North America, Central America and South America.

Something had happened in the sea just near the Atlantic Coast of the Americas.

The sea raced in, engulfing the islands, Porto Rico, Cuba, and getting in North and South America, racing inland for quite a distance.

Yes, it entered in Canada, Mexico and every place, also Brazil and Argentina.

I saw the maps of the Americas, like if they were drawn in the globe, I saw them like if I was very high up in the space. It was very clear. I saw the water going inland, in a BIG wave. I said I felt a lot of interest because the vision was so real and I felt that I was given something for me to understand and see a bit of what is to come.

But the minute I thought that I would see more, the vision finished. I saw enough, however, a big disaster, water taking the Americas, getting in at a high speed.

Source: https://bit.ly/2TTtO49

Myriah Jasmine

Did anyone else have a crazy dream last night? I had a dream that like a huge glowing red and orange fiery asteroid hit the Atlantic ocean by New York and the whole east coast was completely submerged in water and the water was rising because of a tsunami the rock created. The earth shook. It was like a mixture of an asteroid/comet together.

The entire states of Maine, and Florida and the surrounding states were completely submerged in water. Wiped off the map. The ENTIRE EAST COAST was lost underwater and the water just kept rising and rising.

It was vivid and insane and I couldn't wake My self up.

Source: https://bit.ly/2XgJReg

Pamela Banda

I'm from Dallas, so I travel back and forth quite a bit to see family and friends. While I was driving, it must have been early morning time. Traffic was flowing easy. Then all of the sudden I saw water rushing down Highway 45 and immediately by the Spirit I knew it was a Tsunami coming from the Gulf. I knew I was halfway to back to Houston, so I would say Centerville. I had not even reached Houston yet and the water had come that far from the Gulf!

The water was destroying every single car in front of me. When

I saw it coming towards my car, I knew I couldn't escape, but I also knew I was having a vision so I thought for sure I would come out of the vision, but I didn't. The water came inside my car and I yelled, "I Repent! I Repent!"

Source: https://bit.ly/2C2p3iK

Brett Creamer

Back in 2008 I was given a vision that frightened me to my core. My family and I were visiting with my parents in Fort Myers Florida for the weekend. After dinner, we said our goodbyes and hit the road to head back to St. Petersburg which is about an hour and forty-five minutes away. We were on the road for about 15 minutes when my kids fell asleep in the back of the vehicle. My wife said she was going to lay her head back and try to get a quick nap. I looked at my wife and kids and I was so thankful for what God had done in my life and in the life of my family.

As soon as she closed her eyes, I started praying to God. I was telling God how thankful my family and I are for the life He has given us. In the middle of the prayer, I found myself standing in the living room of my home (in Saint Petersburg Florida). Instantly it went from night time on the road to day time in my house. I had no idea what was happening, nor where my family was. I looked around and everything had a tinge of blue to it. The walls shimmered with diamonds of light the way it looks when you are swimming under water in a pool on a sunny day.

At that time, I had no idea where the light reflections were coming from so I scanned the room to try and figure it out. As I looked up, I saw the roof was partially ripped off the North West corner of the house and I could see that the house was actually underwater. The surface of the water looked like it was at least 15 feet above the roof line. Now I saw where the light patterns were coming from. I could see the light streaming down from the surface as it reflected all over the walls of the living room. As I stared in amazement at the scene I was standing in, I was suddenly brought back to where I was praying in my car with my family all around me.

To say I was overwhelmed would be an understatement. I got that dream in 2008. Since then, we moved out of Florida and we moved to Indiana. Sadly, we still own the house in Florida since it is financially under water (no pun intended), but as far as what I saw, it, along with all of Florida, will be destroyed. How can I say that all of Florida will be destroyed? Well, our house in Florida sits on the 2nd highest ground in St. Pete (based on an Army Corp of Engineers survey). Since Florida is predominately flat and my house was about 25 feet under water, I can safely assume that all of Florida will be under water. Since we lived on such high ground, we did not need to purchase flood insurance. Well, my vision told me otherwise. No amount of flood insurance will fix what is coming.

Hurricane 2023 wiped out a lot of Fort Myers

Source: https://bit.ly/2B3hOGE

CHAPTER 8 – WAR IN THE MIDDLE EAST

A major war is coming to the Middle East, and by the time you read this book it may have already begun. As I write this chapter, Israeli Prime Minister Benjamin Netanyahu is pledging to go ahead with his plan to annex large portions of Judea and Samaria, and several of Israel's enemies are promising that there will be a military response if that happens. Of course the region has already been on the precipice of war for many years, and this could potentially be the trigger that finally causes it to happen. We don't know that for sure, but what we do know for sure is that war is coming.

I could have included the prophecies below in the chapter about World War III, but I decided not to do that.

In the chapter about World War III, I want to focus on America's coming military conflict with Russia and China, and so I decided to create an entirely separate chapter for prophecies about Israel and the Middle East.

But I definitely believe that the coming war in the Middle East will be one of the primary factors that ultimately results in the U.S. going to war with both Russia and China. If someone wanted to argue that all of the coming conflicts should be grouped under the banner of "World War III", I wouldn't argue with that one bit.

In Matthew 24, Jesus warned that there will be "wars and rumors of wars" during the period of time just before His return, and we have been watching all of the prophetic chess pieces slowly but surely move into position.

As far as Israel is concerned, many people believe that multiple military conflicts are ahead. There will be times of war and times of "peace", and during one of those times of "peace" a Palestinian state will formally be established. But it won't last for very long before more conflict erupts.

In the end, Israel will emerge victorious, and eventually a Jewish Temple will be built on the Temple Mount in Jerusalem.

But we will also see global hatred for the nation of Israel grow rapidly, and anti-Semitism will reach very frightening levels.

It has been said that Israel is God's timepiece, and the Bible makes it very clear that Israel will play a central role during the events of the last days.

We are right on the verge of the fulfillment of so many ancient prophecies regarding the land of Israel, and the following are a few examples of what some modern prophetic voices have been shown regarding the conflicts which will soon engulf the region...

Dr. Maurice Sklar

There is coming an all out war in the Middle East as the neighboring Arab nations will come against Israel with a sudden missile attack starting from the north with Hezbollah, Lebanon, and Syria. Other Arab nations will join. Israel will be hit from all sides at once and there will be deaths and partial destruction of settlements, smaller cities to the north, and some damage to Tel Aviv and Jerusalem as well. Israel will respond with great force, and limited nuclear weapons will release devastation upon the neighboring countries, particularly Lebanon, Damascus, which will be destroyed completely, and the rest of Syria as well as military strikes into Iran, Gaza, and even northern Egypt/Sinai region.

The resulting shaking of the West will then release a tremendous movement of Jews making aliyah back to Israel. There will no longer be security or stability as it has been up to now in America and Europe. Israel will emerge victorious from this war, but hurt. However, the devastation inflicted upon the attackers will be one hundred times worse. The spoils of this war will include much territory and will force the west to recognize the Holy God of Israel. It will emerge as the only stable country in the region. Many, even millions of Arabs will be killed. Islam will receive a mortal wounding by the Holy God of Israel.

Source: https://bit.ly/3hq4ahE

Sadhu Sundar Selvaraj

On 6 December 2011, at 12:45 PM, I was called by the Lord to come and meet him. This was during the conference that was going on. So I stole myself away from the conference and went to my room. As I entered into my room I saw two mighty angels standing there and they beckoned me to go to the balcony. They said, "The Lord is standing there. Go and meet him there."

So I went to the balcony and I saw the Lord Jesus Christ standing very regally. And he beckoned me, "Come and stand beside Me."

When I stood beside him he said, "Look at my beautiful city."

So I looked around. From the hotel high-rise you can see the nice beautiful city. As I was watching, suddenly there was a huge explosion. A bomb dropped and a building exploded. Another bomb dropped and another building exploded. The whole city was gone up in smoke. Warplanes were flying here and there.

The Lord Jesus said, "My city will suffer the pain of war."

Source: https://bit.ly/3hq4ahE

John Paul Jackson

The day is going to come when Israel will hit Iran. They already have hit…there were mystery explosions that happened. And the Lord told me about this: Israel will one day send rockets into Iran, but before that day happens, there will be other explosions called mystery explosions. And those have happened. But one day it is going to happen and when that takes place and those missiles hit Iran, there's going to be a huge growth of anti-Semitism and everybody's going to blame Israel on the price of gasoline.

Source: https://bit.ly/2YnVRKo

John Paul Jackson

Attacking Iran will cause a panic on the world oil market to blackmail the US and any other country that wants to support Israel. They will blackmail and say they will not continue to give that country oil unless you do not continue to support Israel. So, that will change the petroleum market really quick with what the world sees as a surplus market to a condition that is not that.

Source: https://bit.ly/2XTvnQJ

Pastor TD Hale

I saw an attack on Israel, a heavy attack. No timeline but much weeping as I heard the scripture, "Rachel weeping for her children."

Source: https://bit.ly/30sTSY8

Henry Gruver

"When Israel sends troops into Gaza, it will be a sign the Middle East War has started."

Source: https://bit.ly/2XVGI3V

Sarah Menet

I don't know the countries of the world very well, but as I looked at these lands I instinctively knew what countries they were. I was looking at the Middle East and watched as a missile flew from Libya and hit Israel with a big mushroom cloud. I knew that the missile was actually from Iran but people from Iran had been hiding it in Libya and fired it. I knew that it was a nuclear bomb. Almost immediately missiles started flying from one country to another, quickly spreading to all over the world. I also saw that many nuclear explosions did not come from missiles but from ground bombs of some kind. I knew that in the future there would be a nuclear war throughout the world and this is how it would start.

Source: https://bit.ly/2XNNdpJ

Pastor TD Hale

I turned back to see this pressure cooker again and when I did, it blew apart. It blew up and all the contents within flew across Israel. Whatever it was, the contents stirred up the ancient ones and war broke out. All I could see for miles was war, fighting, bloodshed.

Source: https://bit.ly/2MV16vR

Leslie Johnson

In the night I heard the audible voice of God speak the words: Israel Refuses to Help America. Then I heard the following headlines in my heart. This was the order in which I heard them. Not necessarily the order in which they will happen…

-Israel Refuses Help To America

-Omer Ushers In Palestinian State

-One of America's Greatest Times of Need

-Israel is Attacked, America Sends Troops

-Chaos Reigns As Americans Protest Help to Israel

-"It will start with an Internal Revolution…"

Source: https://bit.ly/3dC4nw1

CHAPTER 9 –
WORLD WAR III

This is one of the most difficult chapters for me to write. I love the United States of America, and I have spent so much of my life trying to do what I can to point this nation back to God. Unfortunately, this nation just keeps getting farther and farther away from God with each passing year. I will elaborate on this much more in a later chapter, but for now I want to make the point that America's future could have been much different if we had made much different choices. Just like with individuals, God gives societies the free will to make their own choices. Sadly, instead of choosing life and blessing, America has chosen death and curses. Our sins have piled up to heaven, and judgment is on the way.

So far in this book, you have read about a series of horrific events which will devastate the United States. But the biggest judgment of all comes at the end.

For decades, God has been showing His servants that World War III is coming, and America is going to lose. As you will see below, the Lord showed Dumitru Duduman that when America "goes to war with China, the Russians will strike without warning". A surprise nuclear attack by the Russians using submarines that suddenly surface just off our coastlines will catch the U.S. completely off guard. On December 14th, 1986, Henry Gruver had a remarkable vision in which he was shown details of this attack...

I was in Wales, on December 14, 1986. I went up on top of the Eagle tower in the Caernarvon Castle. It had eight points on it. Each of the points on it were eroded eagles. This castle was built in the 12th century.

I was overlooking the Irish Sea toward the North Sea. Norway, Sweden, Denmark, the tip of Scotland, Greenland, Iceland in that area. All of a sudden I was up above the earth looking down upon the earth like a glove. As I looked down on the earth, I saw massive amounts of all kinds of ships and airplanes. They were coming from up above Norway, out of this inlet. They headed down between the United States and Europe. They literally covered the whole Atlantic.

Then I wanted to see what was happening to the United States. I looked over on the globe at the United States. I saw coming out of the United States these radio communication towers. I saw the jagged lines like they draw to show that communications are coming out. All of a sudden, as I was looking down on them they began to sprinkle down on the earth like dust. I thought "Oh no! They are not getting through! They are not getting through. They don't know what is happening! They are totally oblivious!

Then I began to see all of these submarines emerging from under the surface. I was surprised at how close they were to our borders! They were in our territorial waters! Then I saw the missiles come out of them! They hit eastern coastal cities of the United States.

I looked over across the country where my family was over in the northwest side and I saw the submarines. I saw the missiles coming out and hitting the western coastal cities.

I cried out and I said, "Oh God! Oh God! When will this be, and what shall be the sign of its coming?"

I heard an audible voice speak to me and say, "<u>When Russia opens her doors and lets the masses go</u>. The free world will occupy themselves

117

with transporting, housing and feeding and caring for the masses, and will let down their weapons and cry peace and safety. Then sudden destruction will come. Then is when it will come."

That was December 14, 1986, Glastnost and Perestroika were unheard of at that time!

Source: https://bit.ly/2CLJeln

In this chapter, you will hear from many other prophetic voices that have also seen this attack.

The U.S. military will be absolutely devastated by this surprise first strike, and that will open the door for a ground invasion.

The Chinese and their allies will invade the U.S. on the west coast, and the Russians and their allies will invade the U.S. on the east coast.

The invaders will not show any mercy whatsoever, and many of those that survived the nuclear attack will wish that they had died because conditions will be so horrific.

If God is calling you to leave the United States, you will want to leave before the surprise nuclear attack happens. Because once the nukes start hitting, it will be too late to go anywhere.

I wish that America's fate would have been much different, but the prophetic voices that have been shown these things are all in agreement…

Dumitru Duduman

Then, the man spoke again, "When America goes to war with China, the Russians will strike without warning."

The other two presidents spoke, "We, too, will fight for you." Each had a place already planned as a point of attack.

All of them shook hands and hugged. Then they all signed a contract. One of them said, "We're sure that Korea and Cuba will be on our side, too. Without a doubt, together, we can destroy America."

The president of Russia began to speak insistently, "Why let ourselves be led by the Americans? Why not rule the world ourselves? They have to be kicked out of Europe, too! Then I could do as I please with Europe!"

Source: https://bit.ly/2B188MU

David Wilkerson

America is going to be destroyed by fire! Sudden destruction is coming and few will escape. Unexpectedly, and in one hour, a hydrogen holocaust will engulf America — and this nation will be no more.

Source: https://bit.ly/3cGPh6N

Evangelist A.A. Allen's 1954 Vision

Then suddenly I saw from the Atlantic and from the Pacific, and out of the Gulf, rocket-like objects that seemed to come up like fish leaping out of the water . High into the air they leaped, each headed in a different direction, but every one towards The U.S. On the ground, the sirens screamed louder. And up from the ground I saw similar rockets begin to ascend. To me, these appeared to be interceptor rockets although they arose from different points all over the U.S. However, none of them seemed to be successful in intercepting the rockets that had risen from the ocean on every side. These rockets finally reached their maximum height, slowly turned over, and fell back toward the earth in defeat. Them suddenly, the rockets which had leaped out of the ocean like fish all exploded at once. The explosion was ear- splitting. The next thing which I saw was a huge ball of fire. The only thing I have ever seen which resembled the thing I saw in my vision was the picture of the explosion of the H-bomb in the South Pacific. In my vision, it was so real I seemed to fell a searing heat from it.

Source: https://bit.ly/2MQnmXK

A Vision Minister A.C. Valdez Had In 1929

Right in the middle of that victory, I stood in 6th Avenue Church one day with the power of God on me. All of a sudden, the ceiling just disappeared. Now when I say vision, my friends, I know that some visions are what the Bible calls "night visions," like in a dream. You will find that in the Bible. Dreams are also called visions. Generally speaking, a vision is differentiated by what you see with your eyes open. That which you see when you are not asleep.

I began to see this vision and the Lord showed me. I looked up, I saw what answers to the description of an I.C.B.M. (Inter-continental Ballistic Missile). Just as real as any picture that you would see, or the real thing, if you've ever seen one of those missiles. It was just as real as you would look upon one if it were right in front of you, two or three feet away.

I saw it! It was passing over a skim of clouds. Not heavy clouds, but a thin skim of clouds. I was standing on the side of this mountain, a residential district. I was looking over into a bay area. It would appear like I was in Berkeley, if you've ever been to Berkeley, and the Berkeley Hills. I was looking into the bay area toward San Francisco. The San Francisco Bay region, that direction. I saw the freeway. I don't say that it was the Oakland freeway that is there today. I don't know where it was, my friends. I do know this, that I was standing on the side of this mountain, overlooking a huge metropolis.

When I saw this missile directed toward the city, and suddenly, being electronically controlled no doubt, it plummeted right down into the city and then exploded. Then I saw the fireball, which answers to the description of what I have seen in a civil defense film release of the first Hydrogen bomb explosion. This happened in 1929! Yet I saw it as clear as I see you here tonight. There was a purpose in it. I have been warning people ever since, that this thing is coming. As the day approaches, my friends, I feel more vibrant than ever before. I have got to bear testimony to what I saw with my eyes!

I have got to warn God's people that they must live in the Spirit, and walk in the Spirit and be filled with the Spirit, if they want God's protection in these last days!

I saw this thing blossom out in all of its beautiful colors. Did you ever see a picture of it? It's a beautiful sight, but a horrible sight. All of the colors of the rainbow you can see in that big ball as it swells out. Then the pressure that it creates following the explosion. It demolishes everything before it. It leaves a crater over 300 feet deep and over 2 miles across. It is capable of destroying a huge metropolis the size of New York City in one blast.

Even though there were no freeways in 1929, I saw freeways. I saw them run and jump in their cars to escape, but there was no escape! I saw the aftermath of this explosion. I saw all of the detail. The Spirit of the Lord picked me up. Like St. Paul, whether in the body or out of the body, I don't know. All I know is, my friends, that God took me, and whisked me across that area where the bomb hit in the midst of that huge metropolis. There was nothing left. The center where it struck was molten, like molten glass. It wasn't until I was carried away beyond the residential area that I began to see any sign of debris.

Finally, I came to what looked similar to snow or sand drifts piled up against the fences and buildings. I saw piles of iron, like broom straw, only much finer than broom straw. It was in piles, and in patterns. Everything completely destroyed! Finally, way, way out, beyond what I felt was the residential area, I began to find signs of human beings, only in pieces. Torsos, heads, hands, arms and legs. They were scattered around everywhere!

The Spirit of the Lord carried me out further. I began to find signs of life. People were running. Everybody was blind. I didn't know in 1929 that if you are 35 miles away from the explosion and you happened to be looking in that direction you would never see again. I didn't know that at that time. Everybody was blind, my friends; they were running and screaming and bumping up against this and that and the other, bouncing back, children blind and screaming, and crying out for their parents, and parents for their children.

The farther I went the more the confusion, and the cries increased! My friends, even tonight, while I am speaking to you, I can hear those cries! I can hear those cries, children and parents screaming out for one another! It was a terrible sight to behold! If I were to live ten-thousand years I know I could just close my eyes, and hear those screams, and see the terror that was written all over the faces of parents and children! A terrible sight indeed!

Source: https://bit.ly/2Yy9rer

Earlene Wallace's 1992 Vision

1992, Vision, Destruction Of America — while praying in the basement of my home, I saw the sky over America fill with MANY black, stealth bombers. There were no markings on any of the planes. Then the scene changed, and I saw nuclear explosions all around me! Then the scene changed AGAIN, and I saw the terrible aftermath of the nuclear holocaust. Not ALL but MUCH of America as we know it today, was destroyed. And AGAIN, for the fourth time, the scene changed, and I saw hoards of oriental soldiers marching through all of the areas of America that had not been bombed. They had bayonets fixed to their rifles, and were destroying EVERYONE AND EVERYTHING in their way. Then the vision ended.

Source: https://bit.ly/2XsuvDK

Monique Bizet

I saw myself sitting up on the bed, and the Lord said: turn to the right, and there was a white board on the wall. On the white board were written two words in red. On the left it said RUSSIA and it was circled in red, and on the right it said USA and circled as well.

The Lord started to speak to me and said: Russia and China will invade the USA when she is at her weakest. When she is at her weakest Russia and China will invade the nation.

The nation will be destroyed. I got the impression in my heart that the nation will be going thru turmoil, that even though we think it's peace and safety now, there is turmoil, division, civil war that will come bringing us to a weak point; and from the outside invasion will come.

Source: https://bit.ly/2Ua6NKv

Dr. Maurice Sklar

Then I saw three giant rocket missiles that took off into the air. Two came from out of the ocean waters, and one came from land and traveled a great distance. All of them blew up in the air one,two, and THREE in the upper atmosphere within five minutes of each other. It was out near space.

They were terrible nuclear bombs. But the last one was the biggest and it created a huge mushroom cloud over the Midwest part of America. Then the ground shook and everything just went black. There wasn't any electric light coming out of any homes.

Then candles began to be lit and fires, and a little light was seen. There were other nuclear explosions, and many people perished throughout the nation. There was just twisted metal and charred debris in cities that once were tall and majestic.

Source: https://bit.ly/2AjCutu

Dr. Maurice Sklar

I saw three terrible nuclear explosions. I believe they were, ...they didn't hit the ground. They talk about the EMP strike. There were 2 of them that came out of the water, out of the ocean, ...must have been from submarines off the coast. I believe it was the west coast. I saw one that looked like an ICBM, a big, big rocket, that took off, and traveled some distance, almost out to space. But these didn't land on the ground, they exploded in the air, over America. There was like,... 1, 2, and the last one was the biggest one. They exploded in the outer atmosphere. And then I saw everything go dark, just like they say about the electricity.

Source: https://bit.ly/2TCTEta

Pastor TD Hale

Bombs had landed everywhere, the land was totally destroyed.

I saw people standing outside their homes weeping, holding onto each other. I saw dead bodies lying around. I heard someone say, "This should never have happened, this should never have happened."

National destruction had hit America. There was no food or water. Everyone was crying. I saw grown men crying and holding their families, begging God for mercy. The trees were all knocked over. Limbs and leaves were all missing from the trees except a few of the main large trunk limbs. As I continued to move across America I saw people running, searching for missing loved ones many seemed to be totally out of their minds!

Source: https://bit.ly/2YfKWCy

Daniel Rodes

I saw many of the cities in America being destroyed completely by fire and massive military artillery. I saw biological and chemical weapons being used on American soil and against her people. In one of these visions, I saw a yellowish, pale, gooey looking substance fill the air with a cloud completely blotting out the sun and multitudes of people were dying on every hand. This, I believe, was a nuclear fallout or a biological or chemical substance, but the Lord didn't explain it to me. It made me feel like panicking, but suddenly I realized it was not affecting me. I don't know if that means the faithful people of God will escape this or not. The Lord did not give me that direction. However, I do feel that we should pray as Jesus admonished us in Luke 21:36."

Source: https://bit.ly/3OBLqpn

Dumitru Duduman

He said, "Remember this, Dumitru. The Russian spies have dis-

TRUMP
gave them the
info

covered where the nuclear warehouses are in America. When the Americans will think that it is peace and safety – from the middle of the country, some of the people will start fighting against the government. The government will be busy with internal problems. Then from the ocean, from Cuba, Nicaragua, Mexico,,.." (He told me two other countries, but I didn't remember what they were.) "…they will bomb the nuclear warehouses. When they explode, America will burn!"

Source: https://bit.ly/3dYJzyS

Dean Odle

The second dream in the last twelve months, I was driving on interstate 85, I am in Auburn Alabama, so I was was on interstate 85 heading towards Montgomery, which is south west. And I was heading there, and I had a clear straight shot, a long… I could see a long way off. In the dream I said, I bet I will see a mushroom cloud in just a few minutes, or in just a moment. It wasn't until 5 seconds later and BOOM…the flash, the cloud, I watched the whole thing go up and roll over. I don't know where it was, I am not quite sure, but I know I was looking west.

Source: https://bit.ly/2WZmHsO

Sarah Menet

As I was looking at the cities of light, I then saw missiles coming and hitting some cities and mushroom clouds started happening all over the United States. Some were from missiles that I knew came from Russia and others were not from missiles, but were from bombs that were already in the United States. They were hidden in trucks and in cars and were exploded.

I specifically saw Los Angeles, Las Vegas and New York hit with bombs. New York was hit with a missile, but I think that Los Angeles was hit by a truck bomb or actually several, because I didn't see any missile. I also saw north of Salt Lake City have a mushroom cloud, a small one, but no missile.

Source: https://bit.ly/2XNNdpJ

Jan Desisto

I found myself walking around the inside of a two story white mansion. Somehow, I knew I was on the west coast. There was a celebration going on, however, I was an observer going unnoticed by the people inside the party. As I walked around the house, I kept saying to myself "everything here is white", the walls were white, the elegant staircase was white, even the marble floor was white.......everything was white. I thought this was rather unusual, white, white, white, I had never seen anything like this before.

Eventually, I decided to walk outside to the gardens. As I walked out onto the beautiful lush green grass I noticed a body of water. I walked closer to the water's edge as I was enjoying the view, all of a sudden I found myself looking into the interior of a submarine! I remember thinking how can I be looking inside a submarine?

I blinked my eyes and with a shocked expression, I locked eyes with a man in naval uniform. He was a Russian naval officer. I don't even know how I knew he was Russian, but I did. He had a lofty attitude about him as well as a smug look on his face.

As he started to move his hand slowly, my eyes followed his movement. That is when I noticed he was standing next to a nuclear missile. He started to lovingly caress the weapon. The missile had "MH 70" painted on the side of it in white. I screamed at him " YOU ARE RUSSIAN" AND THAT IS A KOREAN MISSILE". Inside my head, I quickly thought of the letters and I recalled they were from a downed commercial airplane supposedly taken down by the Russians. He smiled back at me and said " YES, AND WHEN THE USA IS BUSY AND UNSUSPECTING WE WILL ATTACK YOU."

Source: https://bit.ly/2zlACAI

Zelma Kirkpatrick's 1954 Vision

The third week I wakened out of a sound sleep as if someone had shaken me roughly. Then I saw the terrible war. The soldiers were Chinese and a few Russians. They were dressed in red coats and caps and light khaki trousers, almost white. They ran in a sort of hop-skip way, and they squealed as they fought. They looked to be in a fiendish flee. They would plunge their bayonets in the people's belly and rip them up. They were devils. It was fiendish hell turned loose.

Source: https://bit.ly/3hnIJOk

Michelle Walcott

Russia invades us not sure how but I knew they were here to take spoils. They were everywhere. I saw men wearing all black uniforms not sure who they were but I knew in the dream they were foreign.

These were coming up out of the ocean and walking on to shore. They started shooting everyone they saw. It was total terror & chaos, people just being gunned down.

Source: https://bit.ly/2X0InET

Shari Straight

In 2015, Yah told me that the "next war" will involve "ports, drones and submarines" and that was before I heard about drone submarines. I wondered why He said those three words in that order.

Also, in about 1998, I had a vision where Yah took me up into the atmosphere over the US where I could see the entire United States. I saw three missiles launched at us in rapid succession starting with what I thought must be NYC and then followed by attacks on what I thought might be LA or southern California and then lastly, what I thought was Miami. The arch of the missiles started in the ocean. I knew it was a nuclear attack.

Source: https://bit.ly/3eon0Dt

Marty Breeden

Then suddenly coming from the skies there began to be missiles incoming.

Not dozens, not hundreds, but thousands upon thousands!!!

I knew that America was being attacked with overwhelming force!!!

Source: https://bit.ly/2z2dIy2

Nita Johnson

I had been in a time of fasting and prayer about the future of our country. The Lord decided at that time to give me the first of many revelations about our tumultuous future. I saw soldiers from China as they were moving across America. I saw some of them go up a hill to a Christian's home, force the man out of his home and try to make him deny his faith in Christ. When he wouldn't do it, they beat him to death before my eyes. So, I was taught that America will be under siege by China. During the course of that siege, there will be Christians who will give their lives for Christ. [Matthew 24]

Source: https://bit.ly/377nxqN

J. Reg King

In the vision I saw things happening, and understood in my mind, as it was revealed to me, as to the location and who they were.

The Russian forces were coming out of the area of the Bathurst Inlet. I remember how astonished I was, because they were there undetected. They had a large mobile military attack force, with heavy armour.

Then the scene changes and I saw Russian and U.S. fighter planes in aerial combat over the Alsask, Alberta area, which is near the Saskatchewan border. The invasion route was in the general area of the Alberta and Saskatchewan border along 110 degrees longitude. I was very amazed that hostile aircraft could get so near to the U.S. border, and not be detected and intercepted before that time.

Again the scene changes and I realized the enemy land forces to be just north of the 60th parallel, also as yet undetected, and without any resistance from either Canadian or U.S. forces.

The visionary experience was given to me in the late 1940's and I remember my absolute amazement that an enemy could penetrate so far into our beloved Canada and not be detected.

Source: https://bit.ly/3h1BsDp

Robert Highley

About this time it started to get dark as I made my way down the hill and I began to see many lights in the sky that from a distance looked like small golden mushroom caps. As they got closer I realized the lights from the city were reflecting upon these objects which turned out to be parachutes, thousands upon thousands were alighting upon the city. I could see the faces were Asian. To my horror they were firing automatic machine guns as they came closer to the ground. The freeway below came to a complete stop and 5 men stood alone firing back. I could see that there was so little armed resistance that they would surely be killed within a short time against such overwhelming odds. Great fear seized me as I realized this was a land invasion. When I awoke the extreme fear was with still with me as I realized that the dream was so vivid and real that it made waking reality seem pale.

Source: https://bit.ly/2Af7gDY

Monique Bizet

I was elevated in the spirit over the cities in America, observing from an aerial view above the buildings. Everything was in black and white and muted colors.

I could hear very evil military type people planning to bomb and destroy several cities in America. They were saying, "Let's destroy them while they sleep."

Suddenly, I saw hundreds of war planes releasing bombs over America's cities everywhere.

Source: https://bit.ly/3gu5mQu

Katie Troutman

We looked outside and a nuclear explosion had just taken place.

We got our two dogs and began running to the car. I looked in the sky to the left of us and there was a mushroom cloud in the sky. We got into the car and drove to the hospital. They had showers set up outside the main doors for everybody to wash off with before being allowed to come into the hospital.

Source: https://bit.ly/3f4Dh0Q

Sarah Menet

Almost right on top of these mushroom clouds I saw Russian troops invading the United States. I saw them parachuting into a lot of places, primarily from the East Coast. I saw them parachute into Salt Lake City. I also saw Chinese troops invade from the West Coast, near Los Angeles. The people who were still alive started fighting them with their own guns. I didn't see any military.

Source: https://bit.ly/2XNNdpJ

Michael Snyder

6-4-2019

In my dream I was part of a military unit. I do not know for sure that it was an American unit, but that was my impression. We were in military uniforms and we were heavily armed. We were traveling through extremely rocky terrain, and we got to a point where there were extremely jagged rocks on both sides of a river. Asian troops were on the other side of the river, but in my dream their specific nationality was not indicated.

I believe that it was our side that initiated the firing, but the Asian troops started firing back with deadly efficiency. I could see troops on our side being hit. Then my view changed and somehow I could see more Asian troops swimming up the river toward us at an extremely impressive speed. I was stunned at how fast they were swimming, and I had the impression that they were extremely well trained. They emerged from the water simultaneously, and at that same moment the Asian troops on the other side of the river began to advance.

Our troops were overwhelmed, and those that survived started to retreat. In the dream I was a very good runner, and I began running away from the battle at high speed. At one point a couple of us looked back to see if we could regroup at a new position and continue the battle, but it was hopeless. There were way too many Asian troops.

So I started running again, and I was carrying the jacket of one of my comrades. He had also escaped, but I had gotten separated from him. At one point I laid it down in the path, and in my dream I was hoping that he would come along and find it.

In my dream I could run better than the others, and I ultimately survived and made it back to other U.S. forces. Or at least it was my impression that they were U.S. forces.

I do now know if anyone else from my original unit survived. That is where the dream ended.

Source: https://bit.ly/2MNUNKy

Brother Heath

I immediately heard what sounded like Chinese and Russian chatter but then someone was translating afterwards. It seemed like a conversation between military leaders in high command. The translator said, "The Americans are currently in the beginning of an all out civil war. Their leaders are fallen, in turmoil and there is great confusion in their military. No one knows whose in charge right now. No one can authorize the nuclear codes. This is the best time to mobilize our sleeper cells and launch a surprise attack, a pre-emptive strike and an invasion! We've got the best opportunity to take the Americans out in one grand sweep! It's time!"

I then saw bombs beginning to drop with large American cities on fire. I saw America's fragile power grid attacked and brought down. I saw major cities in pitch black darkness. I saw fleets of American ships and fighter planes completely obliterated. I saw Chinese and Russian troops in clockwork droves invading by air, by land and by sea. I saw predator drones large and small being used to destroy crowds of people who had gathered hoping to be saved... but when the drones began shooting, the crowd would try to disperse but most were killed before they could escape.

During the invasion, I saw utter chaos and unbelievable horror all across America's streets. Anarchy and bloodshed, hunger and starvation, people killing people over dwindling food resources. Neighbor was against neighbor, brother against brother, children against their parents, betrayal and horrific atrocities perpetrated over food and water supplies. Mobs of people grouped together ransacking, pillaging and murdering the confused and battered population. It seemed everyone was desperate, without natural affection or compassion. The stronger survivalists preyed on the weak, treating others like zombies and would kill them, along with their children and even babies without batting an eye. Foreign soldiers took part in the terror. The atrocities were worse than any Hollywood apocalyptic portayal with some lawless ones even resorting to cannabalism, like wolves, eating from dead corpses.

The foreign invaders also had no mercy on the population. They contributed to the chaos with their own style of wholesale torture and slaughter. I saw churches filled with families praying inside, set on fire and the people burned alive. Many buildings were burned with those hiding in them. I saw rotting corpses everywhere. I saw America completely destroyed. I saw the Statue of Liberty toppled and then I heard these words, "Babylon, the great has fallen! Her judgement has come in one hour! She has fallen never to rise up again!"

Source: https://bit.ly/3eXcaVh

Marty Breeden

I dreamed that I was at a stranger's house.
The house was fabulous in structure and it was very ornate and it was huge and appeared to be made, not with just great beauty but was also built with seemingly great fortitude.

I saw the gentleman of the house setting in a big easy chair reading a newspaper and the stock market for the day.
As I begin to stroll through the house, I would pass by multiple TVs.
On every TV I would see:
"BREAKING NEWS!" or "SPECIAL REPORT!".

I would stop to listen to the different reporters and they would all be saying the same thing:

"As tensions continue to rise among the nations, one can only hope for the best.
Let us hope cooler heads prevail….. and that there is a quick solution to these rising tensions which seem to be growing by the minute!"

Upon hearing this, I went to the head of the household and I informed him of what I had heard on all of these TVs from multiple reporters and I warned him that he should be preparing his household!

He literally scoffed at me and said:

"These things have been happening for thousands of years! This time will be no different!"

Upon saying this he immediately went back to reading his paper.

It was then that I felt led of the Lord to walk over to this huge window in the house and I immediately began to see what appeared to be large missiles, coming in multiples, yet they also seem to be as though they were Fireballs falling from the sky!!

Wherever they would hit there would be a huge explosion and then an immediate and instantaneous FIRE!!

Before I could even warn the gentlemen of the house again, it was TOO LATE... his house was HIT!

Immediately a fire begin to ravage the house.
I, along with others begin to try to evacuate the house as quickly as possible.
We exited down the back stairs into the basement.
It just so happened that the huge garage doors were all the way open and we looked out upon Devastation that is beyond description!!!

These missiles or fireballs seemed to be coming by the hundreds and the land appeared to be desolate and on fire...EVERYTHING WAS ABLAZE!!

Then, that same gentleman of the house cried out:

"WHY DIDN'T ANYONE WARN US?"

I looked at him solemnly and said:
"SIR!!!...You WERE WARNED, YET YOU CHOSE NOT TO HEED!"

Source: https://bit.ly/3gYuQ96

CHAPTER 10 – PERSECUTION

I know that the things that I am sharing in this chapter are deeply alarming, but it is imperative to understand what is ahead of us. All throughout human history, those that have followed the God of the Bible have been persecuted. We look back today and we marvel at the stories of the brave martyrs that were stoned, beheaded, fed to lions, cut in two, burned alive or killed by the sword. But most of us never stop to consider that we may have to face similar persecution someday.

In recent years, we have really seen the persecution of Christians really ramp up all over the globe. China is cracking down on Christianity like never before, angry mobs are burning churches in India, radical Islamists are savagely butchering Christians in some parts of Africa, believers that are discovered are shipped off to concentration camps in North Korea, and in some Islamic nations in the Middle East it is literally against the law to practice the Christian faith.

Here in the western world, we don't have to face that sort of persecution yet, but at some point that will change in a major way.

In Matthew 24, Jesus specifically warned us that there will be great persecution in the last days...

8 All these are the beginning of sorrows.

9 Then shall they deliver you up to be afflicted, and shall kill you: and ye shall be hated of all nations for my name's sake.

10 And then shall many be offended, and shall betray one another, and shall hate one another.

11 And many false prophets shall rise, and shall deceive many.

12 And because iniquity shall abound, the love of many shall wax cold.

13 But he that shall endure unto the end, the same shall be saved.

14 And this gospel of the kingdom shall be preached in all the world for a witness unto all nations; and then shall the end come.

Are you ready to endure to the end?

You need to have that question settled with yourself right now, because we are moving into a time when being a Christian could very well cost you your life.

There will be great deception during the tremendous chaos that is ahead, and as a result we will even see Christians turning against Christians.

That should never happen, but it will.

Even among believers, hearts are going to grow very, very cold.

And once the Antichrist comes on the scene, those that refuse to worship him will be hunted down like animals. Of course most of the world will eagerly embrace the Antichrist, but true Bible-believing Christians will never worship him or serve him. So true Bible-believing Christians will be relentlessly hunted down, and multitudes will be beheaded. In fact, the Apostle John specifically warns us about this in Revelation 20:4...

And I saw thrones, and they sat upon them, and judgment was given unto them: and I saw the souls of them that were beheaded for the witness of Jesus, and for the word of God, and which had not worshipped the beast, neither his image, neither had received his mark upon their foreheads, or in their hands; and they lived and reigned with Christ a thousand years.

If we are willing to endure to the end, an eternal reward awaits us that no man can ever take away.

So the good news is that we win in the end.

But first we must face the persecution that is ahead of us, and it will be on a level that the world has never seen before.

The following is what some prophetic voices have been shown over the years regarding this coming great persecution...

Augusto Perez

I not only saw what will happen in the future, but I was allowed to experience the great suffering that humanity will have to go through, especially Christians. I sensed their terrible pain and suffering, their agony, martyrdom and the fierce persecution that they will have to endure. Most of the people had no clue that these things were about to happen, until it was too late. When I came out of this vision of the night, I was sobbing in travail and soaking with perspiration. To this day I am affected by what I experienced on that night.

Source: https://bit.ly/2UsCAqc

David Wilkerson

This power will come from persecution. The persecution madness that is coming upon this earth will drive these Christians closer together and closer to Jesus Christ. They will be less concerned about denominational ties and more concerned and emphasis on the coming of Jesus Christ. The Holy Spirit will bring together as one people in all walks of life.

Source: https://bit.ly/2YuS51R

Daniel Rodes

There will be persecution come upon the American people. Some of the so-called Christians will be taken as slaves and put in work camps similar to that of Israel being in Egypt. Because we will not submit ourselves to the right ways of God and because we have taught our church people contrary to the Holy Scriptures, there will be much persecution. Many Christian pastors will be killed and others will be threatened and greatly tortured. I saw mothers crying as they were being tormented and watched their children die before their eyes.

I saw so-called Christians bring great attacks against the holy remnant and I heard the word of the Lord say to me, "Come out from among her, My people." I heard the Spirit say to me over and over again, "If they do not separate themselves from this evil system, they will become a part of the plague that is coming upon the whole world. They will either separate themselves now or they will be separated in eternity." I saw this deception become so great that the American people were calling good, evil and evil, good. The so-called Christian world tried to stop all who would dare to interfere with their evil ways. Some so-called Christians willingly took the mark of the new age system as the right thing to do.

I saw that while the church was facing severe persecution, the Glory of the Lord appeared and great revivals were taking place among the God-fearing children of God. The more persecution that was put upon them, the more they were purified and made holy. When some of the people who were against Christianity saw how the people rejoiced in the time of persecution, they also became Christians and were willing to suffer with the righteous. This persecution was completely destroying denominational differences and the only goal these Christians had was to line up their lives according to the Word of God, instead of their doctrinal opinions. The Lord informed me that He will not come for a church that is in a state of division, but that His believers will be unified in love and compassion and in the knowledge of the Word of God. The Word of the Lord said to me, "I am coming for a church without spot and wrinkle."

Source: https://bit.ly/2BUzUuS

No such Thing

Daniel Rodes

I saw Christians trying to destroy other Christians and I watched in horror as they tried to destroy all the prophets of God and all those who were warning against coming judgment. They were teaching their people not to listen to "prophets of doom," but that Jesus loved them and they would be "raptured" before any evil happened to them. I watched as these people faced severe persecution and judgment that they were promised they would not see. They turned against those who taught them lies and cursed them to their face. Because of this deception, many so-called Christians turned against the true Christians and were ready to destroy anyone who practiced true Christianity.

I saw Christians persecuting each other, lying about each other and falsely accusing each other to such an extent that there was an angry spirit arising within the churches. They openly persecuted those who didn't agree with their traditional standpoint. They were so deceived that they labeled churches who believed they need to live by the Bible way as cults. The churches that were unscriptural and those who were known as cults in the past became an accepted practice. The word of the Lord came to me saying, "You will hear people boldly, violently and with much hostility, accuse the righteous, holy, God-fearing people of being cult members because they believe in holiness." The word of the Lord came to me again saying, "Persecution within the church causes division, confusion and much destruction, but persecution from without that comes from the world brings people together in unity and love and compassion one toward another. For this cause, severe persecution will come upon the American people. Because they willfully chose the way of division rather than unity, I will send persecution that will cause them to either turn against Me or turn to Me.

Source: https://bit.ly/3cqNq6e

Dr. Roxanne Brant's 1973 Vision

Much persecution broke out against Christians who preached the gospel and witnessed. But in the midst of all these calamities, the (true) church of Jesus Christ waxed valiant and became stronger than ever…millions were swept into the kingdom.

Source: https://bit.ly/37s7Vyh

Augusto Perez

I saw the manifestation of the man of sin, and the fierce persecution that he will unleash upon all the Christians on this nation and the whole world, leading to the mark of the beast and all kinds of horrors.

Source: https://bit.ly/3dPDZPe

Dr. Maurice Sklar

I saw what looked like riot police. Like you see sometimes coming in, with helmets on. Some of them had light blue hats or helmets, I am not sure. It didn't look American, it looked like it was more of a UN type of, or international type of thing, I don't know. They started entering into homes, and they gave the people a choice. They came in heavily armed, with machine guns. They said, 'either you, come with us, ...we have a place for you'. They dragged people out of their homes and brought them to these, they looked like concentration camps. But they didn't look like the world war II type. They looked like they were made into that from schools, corporate buildings and warehouses. There were a lot of them. I knew this was happening, not just in America, but this was happening world wide.

Source: https://bit.ly/2TCTEta

Dr. Maurice Sklar

There was this hologram movie kind of....where the antichrist was three dimensional, it was like he was in front of you, but he wasn't. I have never seen technology quite this advanced. They said .... "your going to be alright, we'll take care of you, just bow down on your knees, and receive me". Almost like he's Lord, but he said it in such a way that it didn't seem like a big deal, but it was. They could not touch the person until they got down on their knees. I didn't put that in what I wrote, but when they got down on their knees, then there was this automatic thing that they got stamped. It looked like an electronic tattoo or stamp. I believe in some parts of the world, it was on their forehead, some parts was on their hand. The right hand, but I saw a forehead. And then they went into this room in the back, and they had food and they could eat, they slept, but when they came out, they were like zombies. They had lost their mind, they were in a complete takeover, like "i robot" movie. It was like a taking over of their whole being. They lost their soul. You could tell. Many of them, the ones that were young, the ones that were fit, were immediately brought into the military, this police force, and they were given weapons and they were like zombies, they went out and joined the police that were rounding everyone up.

Source: https://bit.ly/2TCTEta

Evangelist Joan Schmitz

In the next scene I was lifted up by the Spirit, and as I was looking down, I saw people marching in ranks. Their appearance was that of starvation, as they were skin and bones with hollow eyes. As I watched and listened, into my spirit I was reminded of the great persecution of the Jews under Hitler during World War II. As they marched they were singing a song in a language that I was not familiar with. As I listened, I began to sing in the Spirit the same song. At a later time, the Lord showed me that this would be the coming persecution of the Church and the Jews. It was then that the Lord spoke to me saying, "The stage is being set and the curtain is about to rise on the whole new world system, and the money you have will not be worth the paper it's written on."

Source: https://bit.ly/2XTCfzO

Missionary Patti Rowe's 1974 Vision

I saw a church and I then saw gross darkness. I was standing in light but all else around me was black. Out from the blackness, away from the church, I heard voices scoffing and crying out in bitterness and anger saying, "Where is the coming of the Son of Man? Why hasn't He come?" I recognized those voices of people whom I have known; some who had ridiculed me for leaving everything to go abroad with my small sons. They were people who had a form of Godliness but became all wrapped up in materialism and religious works. Now the end was here and they

✓ The Bible says Jesus will judge us according to our deeds. So Religious works are important.

were hopeless and angry at God, because things had not happened as they had expected. They had no faith to anchor them now. They were now scoffing at God. (There had been no pre-tribulation rapture.)

Source: https://bit.ly/2YtCyzA

Michelle Walcott

The answer repeatedly was No, I will follow Jesus Christ my Lord and only him will I bow down to, it made them angry and they began to torture each one. By braking fingers or bashing knee caps. The dream was so vivid and so real I could hear the bones, each one being broken.

When one didn't cry out in pain they would get more angry and more vile and tortuous. This went on it seemed like forever. I remember in the dream praying the whole time asking the Lord.

Please give me strength, strengthen me to be able to stand and not fear what they will do to my body. Let yourself be glorified in me. Don't let me fear Lord, please, I pleaded with him.

Next they came to me and asked me if I would deny Christ and follow the New World Leader, The Worlds Messiah. I looked at them, there were 2 or 3 standing there but 1 right in front of me. I stood silent and they screamed at me in my face and ordered me to deny Christ.

Source: https://bit.ly/2XOInET

Katie Troutman

I was in what looked like a huge warehouse.
It was dark and dingy almost pitch black.
There was a conveyor that went straight up to a tower. It looked

LOST PROPHECIES OF THE FUTURE OF AMERICA

like a guard tower in the middle and to the side of this humongous warehouse room.

There were tons of people packed in there.
It felt like I was around a bunch of criminals.
They were all dirty and they were bloody and maimed.

All of the sudden I was sitting at the top of the guard tower by the conveyor belt. I was sitting on the platform with my knees up to my chest crying because I didn't want to be there.

It felt so dirty and gross. I was scared.

They had people strapped on the conveyor belt coming up one by one and they were beheading them.

I didn't know at the time this was going to become our reality. I was young and just growing in the Lord.

Source: https://bit.ly/37j6yBW

Ken Peters

About six minutes or so later they opened the doors wide open and what I saw made me experience the emptiest feeling I have ever experienced in my whole life. I saw this man that was very big. He was tall like a professional basketball player but was very big like a professional football player. He had a big satin hood over his head with eyeholes to see out.

My wife was in front of me and they began telling her she should renounce her faith and live. Now I realized what was happening because this man was standing there with a huge sword. It was a very frightening looking sword. I saw this table that was a little longer than the average human being and a little bit wider. My wife said she was not going to renounce her faith in Jesus. She began to preach to them powerfully. She began to rebuke the devil. They got angry and strapped her down on this table with her face up. This man was standing behind her with this sword. So he took the sword and chopped her head right off, right in my presence, I saw it.

Source: https://bit.ly/2WZmHsO

Ken Peters

When this man cut my head off I saw that as soon as it touched my neck, the moment the blade touched my neck, I was gone. I felt no death whatsoever. I was standing their holding a person's hand and I was looking down upon the scene. It was very grotesque. My head was cut off and I was bleeding profusely. Even though this hand was holding me up in the air I was actually more interested in seeing me dead then I was interested in the fact I had been delivered from death.

All of a sudden, I looked down and realized it was another one of these rugged hands holding my hand. I looked up and it was the Lord again. It was the Lord Jesus Christ.

Source: https://bit.ly/2WZmHsO

CHAPTER 11 – WHY GOD IS BRINGING JUDGMENT

A lot of people that will be reading this book may not understand why God would allow all of these bad things to happen to America. As Americans, we like to think of our country as the greatest nation on the entire planet, but that hasn't been true for a very long time. Although God has been sending us warnings for decades, our society has continued to run the other direction. Just about every form of evil that you can possibly imagine is absolutely exploding in our society, and it is getting worse with each passing year.

If you doubt this, I would like for you to consider the following facts that I have pulled out of some of the articles that I have published previously...

#1 America has killed more than 60 million children since Roe v. Wade was decided in 1973. The federal government endorses this activity by heavily funding the country's leading abortion provider, and after that abortion provider harvests the organs of the dead children, the federal government also heavily funds the research that is conducted on those harvested organs.

#2 According to a Quinnipiac University poll, 63 percent of all Americans want to keep Roe v. Wade in place.

#3 Americans are now more likely to die from an opioid overdose than they are from a car accident.

#4 In the city of Baltimore, approximately one out of every four babies is born as an opioid addict.

#5 Overdosing on drugs has now become the leading cause of death for Americans under the age of 50.

#6 The proportion of the U.S. population that dies from drug overdoses is at an all-time high.

#7 The proportion of the U.S. population that experiences alcohol-related deaths is at an all-time high.

#8 The suicide rate in the U.S. is at an all-time record high.

#9 McDonalds feeds approximately 70 million people a day globally. Pornhub gets more than 78 million visits a day.

#10 The teen birth rate in the United States is higher "than in any other industrialized country in the world".

#11 According to the CDC, approximately 110 million Americans have a sexually-transmitted disease.

#12 According to the United Nations Population Fund, 40 percent of all births in the U.S. now happen outside of marriage. But if you go back to 1970, that figure was sitting at just 10 percent.

#13 At this point, approximately one out of every three children in the United States lives in a home without a father.

#14 Approximately one-fourth of the entire global prison population is in the United States.

#15 By the time an American child reaches the age of 18, that child will have seen approximately 40,000 murders on television.

#16 According to the Centers for Disease Control and Prevention, doctors in the United States write more than 250 million prescriptions for antidepressants each year.

#17 Over half a million people are homeless in the United States right now, but more cities than ever are passing laws making it illegal to feed them.

#18 One study found that the average American spends 86 hours a month on a cell phone.

#19 A different study found that one-third of all American teenagers haven't read a single book in the past year.

#20 According to a study conducted by the Centers for Disease Control and Prevention, approximately two-thirds of all Americans in the 15 to 24-year-old age bracket have engaged in oral sex.

#21 It has been reported that one out of every four teen girls in the U.S. has at least one sexually transmitted disease.

#22 It has been estimated that 30 percent of all Internet traffic now goes to adult websites.

#23 According to the Pentagon, 71 percent of our young adults are ineligible to serve in the U.S. military because they are either too dumb, too fat or have a criminal background.

#24 The city of San Francisco handed out a total of 5.8 million free syringes to drug addicts in just one 12 month period.

#25 During one seven day stretch, a total of 16,000 official complaints were submitted to the city of San Francisco about piles of human feces littering the streets.

#26 When you include unfunded liabilities, the true size of our national debt is now over 200 trillion dollars. What we are doing to future generations of Americans is beyond criminal.

#27 There are more than 850,000 registered sex offenders in the United States today.

#28 The number of American babies killed by abortion each year is roughly equal to the number of U.S. military deaths that have occurred in all of the wars that the United States has ever been involved in combined.

#29 About one-third of all American women will have had an abortion by the age of 45.

#30 One very shocking study found that 86 percent of all abortions are done for the sake of convenience.

#31 An average of more than 100 churches are dying in the United States every single week.

#32 Only about 27 percent of all U.S. Millennials currently attend church on a regular basis.

#33 The number of Americans with "no religion" has increased by more than 260 percent over the last three decades.

Just like with individuals, God gives societies a choice.

America could have chosen to follow God's ways, and we would have been greatly blessed if we had chosen that path.

But instead we have chosen to reject God's ways and have chosen to endlessly indulge in every form of sin imaginable.

It has gotten to the point where evil is called good and good is called evil, and anyone that tries to stand up for righteousness is considered to be the enemy.

God has been so patient with America, and He has sent so many of His servants to try to call the United States back to repentance, but the American people do not want to listen to such warnings.

In fact, even the vast majority of the churches in the U.S. want absolutely nothing to do with such warnings.

As we have seen at other times throughout human history, there is only so much time before judgment eventually comes.

At one time America was a great light to the rest of the world and we sent armies of missionaries all over the planet. But now the only example we are setting for the rest of the world is a bad one, and sin has become our greatest export.

Great judgment is coming, and our nation deserves every ounce of it. If only we had repented and turned back to God, things could have been so different. But that did not happen, and prophetic voices all over the world have been shown that America's end will be a very bitter one…

David Wilkerson

America has sinned against the greatest light. Other nations are just as sinful, but none are as flooded with gospel light as ours. God is going to judge America for its violence, its crimes, its backsliding, its murdering of millions of babies, its flaunting of homosexuality and sadomasochism, its corruption, its drunkenness and drug abuse, its form of godliness without power, its lukewarmness toward Christ, its rampant divorce and adultery, its lewd pornography, its child molestations, its cheatings, its robbings, its dirty movies, and its occult practices. In one hour it will all be over. To the natural mind it is insanity to come against a prosperous, powerful nation and cry out, 'It's all over! Judgment is at the door! Our days are numbered!' The Church is asleep, the congregations are at ease, and the shepherds slumber. How they will scoff and laugh at this message. Theologians will reject it because they can't fit it into their doctrine. The pillow prophets of peace and prosperity will publicly denounce it.

Source: https://bit.ly/3eSdwk6

Daniel Rodes

I heard the screaming and crying of the little children as they were being torn to pieces in abortion clinics. The word of the Lord came to me and said that the blood of the millions of innocent children is crying out from the ground for vengeance. Because of the shedding of blood, there will be many lives lost in exchange for this innocent blood being shed.

Source: https://bit.ly/2MmW7E0

Dumitru Duduman

He showed me all of California and said, "This is Sodom and Gomorrah! All of this, in one day it will burn! It's sin has reached the Holy One." Then he took me to Las Vegas. "This is Sodom and Gomorrah. In one day it will burn." Then he showed me the state of New York. "Do you know what this is?" he asked. I said, "No." He said "This is New York. This is Sodom and Gomorrah! In one day it will burn." Then he showed me all of Florida, "This is Florida." he said. "This is Sodom and Gomorrah! In one day it will burn."

Source: https://bit.ly/3dYJzyS

Sadhu Sundar Selvaraj

Then on 20 June (the next day) at 6:45 in the evening, a mighty angel appeared in my room with a scroll in his hand. He unfolded the scroll and he began to read, "These people, Americans, have been marked for destruction." *Yellowstone (?)*

When he spoke those words, I saw angels, many of them in many places all over the United States, standing ready to execute destruction upon the nation. I saw three places that were marked for massive destruction through earthquakes. I don't know what are the three places. I was just shown three places. So, I did some googling and found there are three major fault lines in the United States. One is the San Andreas and the other is in the middle of the United States and the third is somewhere else.

Again, I asked the same thing, "Why must you do this?"

The angel told me, "Son of Man, these people are wicked and obstinate, worse than Nineveh and Sodom and Gomorrah."

So, when I tried to appeal, this is what they are saying, "Why are you asking all this? Don't you know? These people are very wicked and very obstinate and they are worse than the people of Nineveh and Sodom and Gomorrah."

Source: https://bit.ly/3gZ4bJ5

John Paul Jackson

The shape of the United States will change if we do not cry out to God. See here's why. You say, "Why is all this happening?" It boils down to the Garden of Eden and that is this: whenever man fell away from God, he began to decay. Everything he touched began to decay. The Lord said it kind of like this, "And the earth will longer yield itself to you."

Source: https://bit.ly/2YnVRKo

Dr. Samuel Doctorian's 1998 Vision

From the east of the U.S.A. to California. I saw in his hand a bowl. The angel said he would pour out over these countries the judgments that were in the bowl. Then I heard the angel say, "No justice anymore. No righteousness. No holiness. Idolatry. Materialism. Drunkenness. Bondage of sin. Shedding of innocent blood – millions of babies being killed before they are born. Families are broken. An adulterous generation. Sodom and Gomorrah is here. The days of Noah are here. False preachers. False prophets. Refusing of my love. Many of them have the imitation of religion, but denying the real power.

Source: https://bit.ly/3cTUl8h

Matthew Stephen

The man on the white horse said, "On this day a great woe has come upon this union and in the last day it will come again and we who fight today will die tomorrow and this union will be lost." Then a number of troops and horses were brought in. Seven large cannon's were set up in front of the Capitol building and a white dove flew around the top of the capitol. The dove cried out in a loud voice, "You shall stand as long as you worship the Lord God Almighty, but know this," I heard a sound in the distant time, "It has been declared and your time has been weighed; when you come to your last days you have been found wanting. In the end your union shall not stand because you have forgotten The Almighty God".

Source: https://bit.ly/2A6ftuy

Diana Pulliam

In an open vision, I was moving through the streets of a heavily populated city. It was dark, and I seemed to be in the downtown area. I can't say which city, because I was only looking down at the streets. The streets were filled with blood! The blood was at least a few inches deep. A gigantic mop was swishing back and forth through the streets, like it was cleaning up the mess. I heard the Lord say:

"I have to cleanse the land. Blood covers this land."

I began to see faces and bodies. They were covered in blood. Some were screaming for help; others were face down in the blood. The Lord impressed upon me that some of the dead will be people we know. I won't describe the rest of what I saw, but it was like a massacre had taken place. And then He said,

"The land must be cleansed. Much blood has been shed. You MUST trust Me in this. I Am a Righteous Judge."

Source: https://bit.ly/3fknDyp

Jeremiah Johnson

"I am releasing apostolic and prophetic messengers who will trumpet my end-time judgments to the church and warn of the consequences of those who only know the Lamb of mercy and grace, but reject the Lion of judgment and wrath.

Many only know Me as the great intercessor, which I am, but I am also the coming King and judge. There is more than intercessory prayer. For I will teach My people in these last days how to pray kingly and judicial prayers. I will establish My government in the earth and make My enemies a footstool. I will rule and reign with an iron scepter.

Jeremiah, many will be offended at My return! They have created a god in their own likeness and image and will deny Me when I come with all My glory, power and splendor! You must warn the church of the scoffing spirit that will come, of the overemphasis of My goodness and never teaching on My severity, of never proclaiming and warning of My wrath and judgment that is here now and is yet to come."

The look in the Lord Jesus Christ's eyes as He said these words to me was so intense, yet so deeply grieved. He then asked me if He could entrust me with these words, and I said yes. When I did, He turned around and vanished from my bedroom.

Source: https://bit.ly/2UCkvWw

Dumitru Duduman

"Get up! I want to show you the judgment of the people and the wicked. But the hardest judgment will be received by the church because they knew My word and My power, but many of them dishonored Me, giving into defilement, adulteries, wickedness, and dishonored My name before men who did not know Me. For this, I am filled with rage, and I have been given the authority to take revenge against the inhabitants of the earth – those who have dishonored Me."

Source: https://bit.ly/2A5K9Mt

As I close this chapter, I would like to share something from John Paul Jackson.

In 2012, he gave an update on what the Lord was revealing to him regarding the "perfect storm" that was coming to America. From time to time, the Lord would show him a newspaper headline from the future, and one evening he decided to share many of those headlines with all of us. Some of these headlines have already been fulfilled or are in the process of being fulfilled, while others are still for a future time...

-Too Big to Fail – Fails – Nations Bank being pushed

-Decay in America – Is the Infrastructure of America beyond repair?

-The Rise and Fall of the political parties – New third party gains ground

-The Washington Monument tilts more, Delays announced to other Monument repairs

-The Great divide – The new Normal on the Mississippi River

-Washington DC Riots continue

-Chicago up in Arms – Death Toll Mounts

-Where is The Navy – Why didn't we See it Coming?

-New United America being Pushed – Canada, Mexico, USA in Talks

-GPS loses it GPS – How Long Until We Know Where We Are?

-Three Planes down from Solar Tsunami – Search Continues

-Volcano Erupts Near Tokyo, 7 Million Dead, Another Million Missing

-City Tunnels Closed after bomb

-New Years Terror – Out With the New, in With the Old

-Record Set for Number of Cities with Riot Curfews

-Martial Law to be extended for 30 More Days

-Military Cuts Number of Soldiers

-Nuclear Disaster Under the High Seas

-Ocean Temperature Rise Spreading – Millions of fish dying

-Blight in Grains Spreading

-Drought Continues to cause Prayer to Rise

-NFL Postpones all Games Until Answer Found

-Does God Play Softball? – Hail the size of softballs destroy thousands of homes and Autos

-The North Pole is Now Found in North Russia

-Cyber Attack Cripples Grid – Multiple Collapses with Restart Efforts

-More Explosions in Tel Aviv – Radioactive traces found

-Politics and Trust the new Oxymoron

-What other Secret Weapons Does Israel Have? – Has Israel Played all it's Cards?

-Loss of Identity – The Cost to Belong to the New Euro Community

-Radical Solutions Create Shockwave – Administration says, "We Ran Out of Answers"

-Israel says if Missiles hit Jerusalem, Mecca will be hit within minutes

-Record High Temps Accompany Record Drought Swept South

-Demand for Classic Seeds Skyrocket

-Derivative Panic Hits Global Markets

-Food Prices Lead Nation's Escalating Inflation Woes

-Sysco Co and Kraft Considers Guards on Delivery Trucks as Food Nears 40% of the Family Budget

-Big Regulations Hit Small Banks

-Credit Markets Freeze Up

-The New Face of Robinhood – Flash Mobs Loot Rich Neighborhoods

Source: https://bit.ly/2YphLgs

What has happened to America should deeply sadden all of us.

The mainstream media tells us that liberals won "the culture war", but the truth is that we all lost.

God is going to have the final say, and the great evil that we have chosen will result in the destruction of our nation.

That doesn't mean that all hope is lost. In fact, in a later portion of this book I am going to explain why you can personally have great hope during these troubled times.

But the only hope for America as a whole was repentance, and that never happened.

We should mourn for what was lost, and it is appropriate to grieve as each judgment comes, but God will also be moving greatly even during these exceedingly dark times.

Even in the midst of all the chaos and darkness, the greatest move of God in the history of the world is coming, and that is the topic that we will explore in the next chapter.

CHAPTER 12 – THE GREATEST MOVE OF GOD

When we discuss Bible prophecy and the events of the last days, there can be a tendency to focus on all of the bad things that are going to happen, and it is definitely true that we are going to witness all sorts of things that are truly horrific. In fact, the Bible says that there has never been a time like it before, and there will never be a time like it again.

However, not everything will be bad. In fact, I believe that we are on the verge of the greatest move of God in all of human history.

Even in the midst of all the chaos and darkness that are coming, God is going to be pouring out His Spirit and doing things that are absolutely unprecedented. Prophetic voices all over the globe have been shown this great revival that is coming, and it is going to absolutely shake the entire planet.

For decades, many have been praying for revival, and we are the generation that is going to see it. Men and women around the world have been taken through times of great testing and times of great trials so that they might be ready to prepare the way for the return of the Lord. A lot of believers that felt sidelined by the institutional church system are about to realize that they have been given a mission that is bigger than they ever imagined.

I have no idea why you originally bought this book, but it is not a mistake that you are reading it. You were meant to hear this message, and in many of you it will light a great fire in your heart. God has a purpose for you, and for many of you that are reading this that might be the main reason why the Lord led you to get this book.

In 1961, Tommy Hicks had a vision of multitudes being anointed for a "mighty end-time ministry", and David Wilkerson saw the rise of a "supernatural invisible church". In these last days, true believers are going to come together in unity, and we are going to see things restored to the way that they were during the days of the very first Christian believers.

For years, I have been proclaiming that God is raising up the Remnant of the last days, and this message has resonated with people all over the planet.

And we know with 100 percent certainty that this Remnant will exist in the last days, because the Bible tells us that it will.

Revelation 12:17 tells us the following about this Remnant…

And the dragon was wroth with the woman, and went to make war with the remnant of her seed, which keep the commandments of God, and have the testimony of Jesus Christ.

And in case we missed it the first time, Revelation 14:12 once again identifies this group of believers as those "that keep the commandments of God, and the faith of Jesus"…

Here is the patience of the saints: here are they that keep the commandments of God, and the faith of Jesus.

A Remnant is rising that will keep God's commandments, that will preach the gospel to the entire world and bring in the greatest harvest of souls in all of human history, and that will move and grow in all the fruit, all the gifts and all the power of the Holy Spirit like we haven't seen since the Book of Acts.

I believe that the greatest chapter for the people of God will be the last chapter, and you can be a part of it.

If that doesn't get you excited, I don't know what will.

You may have thought that you would never get to do anything truly special with your life, but unless you are already dead and buried your life is not over.

There is a reason why God put you at this particular time in history, and you have a job to do. But it is up to you whether you will accept that mission or not.

As I keep telling people, there is no other time in all of human history that I would have rather lived than right now. The greatest outpouring of the Holy Spirit that the world has ever experienced is coming, and God has been showing this to His servants all over the world...

David Wilkerson

I see the rise of a super church, a supernatural invisible church, a union of deeply spiritual followers of Jesus Christ, bound together through the Holy Spirit and mutual confidence in Christ and in his word.

This supernatural church of true believers will become a kind of underground church. It will include Catholics and Protestants of all denominations, young and old, black and white, and people of all nations.

Source: https://bit.ly/2YuS51R

Evangelist Bobby Martz

The Lord brought me back to the people that had been weeping before the Lord for the nations. I saw these people stand on their feet. They turned around. They were facing the world in terrible, terrible conditions. The darkness that was upon the earth was horrible, indescribable. It was terrifying; but these people that had been interceding and weeping, the amazing thing was, they were not afraid. They were not afraid of what they were looking at. They were not afraid of the terrible gross darkness. They were full of the Holy Spirit. They began to go forward as one, united. They began to speak the Word of God. The gospel was coming out of their mouths. They were speaking to the multitudes in darkness before them. I saw the Holy Spirit bringing multitudes and multitudes of people into the Kingdom of God in the last days. There were so many people coming to Jesus that I could not see the end. It was a huge, huge multitude of people coming into the Kingdom of God.

Source: https://bit.ly/36XgWiY

Pastor TD Hale

I heard a Voice say, "Pick up the mantle of prayer. Cover yourself with it and find you a secret place to cover my servants in prayer. Many eyes have been anointed with a special anointing to see. Others are blinded to My Word. All things will be revealed in their due course.

A supernatural wave of My Spirit will come over this generation soon. The FINAL voices are in the land to speak one last time. Think it not strange the happenings around you. They must and will come to pass, but I have placed in your hands: the food to sustain you in the months ahead. I have spoken and shown the matter. Tell my servants, saith the Lord, there is coming harsh days ahead!"

Source: https://bit.ly/2YfKWCy

Dr. Maurice Sklar

Revival broke out, and great evangelists and prophets and apostles rose up and began to preach to thousands out doors, and many were saved and were born again. Miracles of provision, multiplication of food and water, and astonishing healings occurred.

Source: https://bit.ly/2AjCutu

Ken Peters

I did not see any big-name evangelist or prophets or apostles or famous television personalities, Not one. All I saw was every day normal children of God ministering in the power like Jesus described in the Bible with the disciples. This was happening on a wholesale basis, everywhere! People were praying for sick people and they would be healed instantly. They would pray for blind eyes and they would be opened. They would pray for dead people and they would be resurrected. They were praying for the lost to come in. What I saw was the greatest thing I have ever witnessed since I have been alive. Nothing I have ever witnessed on earth could compare to what I was allowed to see.

Source: https://bit.ly/328Py13

Dr. Maurice Sklar

I saw these big outdoor meetings, where God had risen up these end times prophets and apostles, and there was amazing miracles of food and water. What struck me was there was NO FOOD AND WATER. People were starving. People would get to these refuge places .....big fields, and they would see awesome miracles, healings and creative things.

Source: https://bit.ly/2TCTEta

Marty Breeden

During this chaos, there was also a mighty move of God. Many were moved by fear and because they were seeing the fulfillment of things they heard as a child, so they came broken to the Lord and He welcomed them in! I saw many ministers of God during this time walking in wisdom and in great power and authority. I saw spontaneous church services, preaching in parking lots, and supernatural moves of God, often in homes.

Source: https://bit.ly/37u8WWW

Dr. Jonathan Hansen

During this time, these servants of God will do great exploits. The supernatural manifestations of the true and living God will be evidenced to the world and the greatest revival since mankind began will be unleashed with signs and wonders, healing and salvation, but also, the greatest persecution of believers will be taking place with Christians being arrested, imprisoned and killed.

Source: https://bit.ly/3iF9IWh

Sarah Menet

As I looked upon the scene of chaos, destruction and smoke, I noticed that there were these little pockets of light scattered all over the United States. There were, I would guess, about twenty or thirty of them. I noticed that most of these places of light were in the western part of the United States, with only three or four in the East.

These places of light seemed to shine through the darkness and caught my attention and so I concentrated on them, asking, "What are these things?"

I could then see that they were people who had gathered together and they were on their knees and they were praying. The light was coming from them and I understood that it represented their goodness and love. I understood that they had gathered together for safety and that they cared more for each other than for themselves. Some of the groups were small, with only a hundred people or so, but in other groups there were what seemed several thousand.

Source: https://bit.ly/2XNNdpJ

Sadhu Sundar Selvaraj

I saw a group of people especially young people they're all in hiding. They have nothing to eat. I saw a youth and he appeared like a youth leader, he was leading a group of youths and they were all hungry. He just pointed his finger at the ground and he commanded food to grow. And it grew!! Like food hidden in the ground. It grew then it came out they took and the ate. He spoke to a storm a rock and it gave out water. You see, the God who was with Moses is still alive on the throne as He was with the prophet Moses so will he be with you in these last days.

Source: https://bit.ly/3ehiqGA

Dr. Maurice Sklar

There is a new generation of prophets about to emerge. They will operate in the miraculous to such an extent that they will confound the unbelieving and smash the idols of this modern age. They will release both supernatural blessings upon My bride as well as unleashing my judgment upon the earth. No one will be able to ignore them. They will emerge both from the church and out of the remnant of faithful, believing Jews. I have begun already to release the mantles of the Endtime ministry of Elijah for the church age. I will release the ministry of creative miracles and the raising of the dead. No disease shall be able to stand in the presence of My last-day prophets.

Source: https://bit.ly/3gKzNBj

Hollie L. Moody

I turned and watched as the two groups of people converged on the nations of the world.

I watched as one group brought healings, restoration, hope, etc., to the people of the nations who loved the Lord. I watched as things that had been broken down were built back up by them. I saw as some of the people from the wilderness cast out nets into the oceans of the world, and when they drew the nets back to shore, had gathered the souls of the lost. This scene thrilled my heart.

I also observed as the other group of people, with their axes and/or weapons of warfare, fought against those who refused to submit to the authority of the Lord God. All that was against the Lord, was hewn down. These scenes filled me with dread.

"What is this all about, Lord?" I asked the Lord.

The Lord turned and answered me. "These are prophets of the Highest, messengers of My covenant," He said to me. "I have prepared them, proved them and known them in their time in the wilderness. They go before Me to prepare the way for My return. And truly, child, My return is near; even at the doors."

Wordlessly, I turned and once again began to watch the messengers of the covenant as they went forth into the world with their message from the Lord.

Source: https://bit.ly/36KnrWg

Nita Johnson

Then the vision changed and I saw a huge brick oven – a sort of kiln – one that would be used for baking pottery in perhaps the early 1800's. In looking closer, instead of potter, I saw silver vessels being fired.

I asked the Lord what the silver vessels were. I than saw a man's arm reach in with a long shovel-like instrument to take the silver vessels out. The Lord replied, "These are they whom I am releasing at this time for front-line ministry."

I found myself strangely drawn back to again peer into the huge oven. I said, "Lord, what are those vessels way back in the back? Do you see them, Lord? I can just barely see them. They seem almost hidden back on a shelf in the back of the oven.

The Lord then replied, "Those are my golden vessels. I am keeping them hidden in the fiery furnace until the time of their appearing. Only silver vessels will be revealed at this time. The golden vessels will be released soon after their great fiery trial." The vision came to an end.

When I saw these prophets coming and saw the Church's fear, I couldn't help but ask Him, "Lord, why does the Church so fear these awesome men?" "They will bear the rod of government – a seemingly unbearable yoke to the Church." I saw and felt the power and unparalleled authority flowing out of these golden vessels. I felt the holy fear of God which emanated from them, and I instinctively knew that the apostle would bear a rod of government of even greater proportion. The Lord then concluded by saying, "The Church greatly fears their coming."

Source: https://bit.ly/3dsSoRl

The Full Text Of A Vision Evangelist Tommy Hicks Was Given In 1961

My message begins July 25, about 2:30 in the morning at Winnipeg, Canada. I had hardly fallen asleep when the vision and the revelation that God gave me came before me. The vision came three times, exactly in detail, the morning of July 25, 1961. I was so stirred and so moved by the revelation that this has changed my complete outlook upon the body of Christ, and upon the end time ministries.

The greatest thing that the church of Jesus Christ has ever been given lies straight ahead. It is so hard to help men and women to realize and understand the thing that God is trying to give to his people in the end times.

I received a letter several weeks ago from one of our native evangelists down in Africa, down in Nairobi. This man and his wife were on their way to Tanganyika. They could neither read nor could they write, but we had been supporting them for over two years. As they entered into the territory of Tanganyika, they came across a small village. The entire village was evacuating because of a plague that had hit the village. He came across natives that were weeping, and he asked them what was wrong.

They told him of their mother and father who had suddenly died, and they had been dead for three days. They had to leave. They were afraid to go in; they were leaving them in the cottage. He turned and asked them where they were. They pointed to the hut and he asked them to go with him, but they refused. They were afraid to go.

The native and his wife went to this little cottage and entered in where the man and woman had been dead for three days. He simply stretched forth his hand in the name of the Lord Jesus Christ, and spoke the man's name and the woman's name and said, "In the name of the Lord Jesus Christ, I command life to come back to your bodies." Instantaneously these two heathen people who had never known Jesus Christ as their Savior sat up and immediately began to praise God. The spirit and the power of God came into the life of those people.

To us that may seem strange and a phenomenon, but that is the beginning of these end-time ministries. God is going to take the do-nothings, the nobodies, the unheard-of, the no-accounts. He is going to take every man and every woman and he is going to give to them this outpouring of the Spirit of God.

In the book of Acts we read that "In the last days," God said, "I will pour out my Spirit upon all flesh." I wonder if we realized what he meant when God said, "I will pour out my Spirit upon all flesh." I do not think I fully realize nor could I understand the fullness of it, and then I read from the book of Joel: "Be glad then, ye children of Zion, and rejoice in the Lord your God: for he hath given you the former rain moderately, and he will cause to come down for you the rain, the former rain, and the latter rain" Joel 2:23. It is not only going to be the rain, the former rain and the latter rain, but he is going to give to his people in these last days a double portion of the power of God!

As the vision appeared to me after I was asleep, I suddenly found myself in a great high distance. Where I was, I do not know. But I was looking down upon the earth. Suddenly the whole earth came into my view. Every nation, every kindred, every tongue came before my sight from the east and the west, the north and the south. I recognized every country and many cities that I had been in, and I was almost in fear and trembling as I beheld the great sight before me: and at that moment when the world came into view, it began to lightning and thunder.

As the lightning flashed over the face of the earth, my eyes went downward and I was facing the north. Suddenly I beheld what looked like a great giant, and as I stared and looked at it, I was almost bewildered by the sight. It was so gigantic and so great. His feet seemed to reach to the north pole and his head to the south. Its arms were stretched from sea to sea. I could not even begin to understand whether this be a mountain or this be a giant, but as I watched, I suddenly beheld a great giant. I could see his head was struggling for life. He wanted to live, but his body was covered with debris from head to foot, and at times this great giant would move his body and act as though it would even raise up at times. And when it did, thousands of little creatures seemed to run away. Hideous creatures would run away from this giant, and when he would become calm, they would come back.

All of a sudden this great giant lifted his hand toward the heaven, and then it lifted its other hand, and when it did, these creatures by the thousands seemed to flee away from this giant and go into the darkness of the night.

Slowly this great giant began to rise and as he did, his head and hands went into the clouds. As he rose to his feet he seemed to have cleansed himself from the debris and filth that was upon him, and he began to raise his hands into the heavens as though praising the Lord, and as he raised his hands, they went even unto the clouds.

Suddenly, every cloud became silver, the most beautiful silver I have ever known. As I watched this phenomenon it was so great I could not even begin to understand what it all meant. I was so stirred as I watched it, and I cried unto the Lord and I said, "Oh, Lord, what is the meaning of this," and I felt as if I was actually in the Spirit and I could feel the presence of the Lord even as I was asleep.

And from those clouds suddenly there came great drops of liquid light raining down upon this mighty giant, and slowly, slowly, this giant began to melt, began to sink itself in the very earth itself, and as he melted, his whole form seemed to have melted upon the face of the earth, and this great rain began to come down. Liquid drops of light began to flood the very earth itself and as I watched this giant that seemed to melt, suddenly it became millions of people over the face of the earth. As I beheld the sight before me, people stood up all over the world! They were lifting their hands and they were praising the Lord.

At that very moment there came a great thunder that seemed to roar from the heavens. I turned my eyes toward the heavens and suddenly I saw a figure in white, in glistening white–the most glorious thing that I have ever seen in my entire life. I did not see the face, but somehow I knew it was the Lord Jesus Christ, and he stretched forth his hand upon the nations and the people of the world — men and women — as he pointed toward them, this liquid light seemed to flow from his hands into them, and a mighty anointing of God came upon them, and those people began to go forth in the name of the Lord.

I do not know how ling I watched it. It seemed it went into days and weeks and months. And I beheld this Christ as he continued to stretch forth his hand; but there was a tragedy. There were many people as he stretched forth his hand that refused the anointing of God and the call of God. I saw men and women that I knew. People that I felt would certainly receive the call of God. But as he stretched forth his hand toward this one and toward that one, they simply bowed their head and began to back away. And each of these that seemed to bow down and back away, seemed to go into darkness. Blackness seemed to swallow them everywhere.

I was bewildered as I watched it, but these people that he had anointed, hundreds of thousands of people all over the world, in Africa, England, Russia, China, America, all over the world, the anointing of God was upon these people as they went forward in the name of the Lord. I saw these men and women as they went forth. They were ditch diggers, they were washerwomen, they were rich men, they were poor men. I saw people who were bound with paralysis and sickness and blindness and deafness. As the Lord stretched forth to give them this anointing they became well, they became healed, and they went forth!

And this is the miracle of it — this is the glorious miracle of it — those people would stretch forth their hands exactly as the Lord did, and it seemed as if there was this same liquid fire in their hands. As they stretched forth their hands they said, "According to my word, be thou made whole."

As these people continued in this mighty end-time ministry, I did not fully realize what it was, adn I looked to the Lord and said, "What is the meaning of this?" And he said, "This is that which I will do in the last days. I will restore all that the cankerworm, the palmerworm, the caterpillar — I will restore all that they have destroyed. This, my people, in the end times will go forth. As a mighty army shall they sweep over the face of the earth."

As I was at this great height, I could behold the whole world. I watched these people as they were going to and fro over the face of the earth. Suddenly there was a man in Africa and in a moment he was transported by the Spirit of God, and perhaps he was in Russia, or China or America or some other place, and vice versa. All over the world these people went, and they came through fire, and through pestilence, and through famine. Neither fire nor persecution, nothing seemed to stop them.

Angry mobs came to them with swords and with guns. And like Jesus, they passed through the multitudes and they could not find them, but they went forth in the name of the Lord, and everywhere they stretched forth their hands, the sick were healed, the blind eyes were opened. There was not a long prayer, and after I had reviewed the vision many times in my mind, and I thought about it many times, I realized that I never saw a church, and I never saw or heard a denomination, but these people were going in the name of the Lord of Hosts. Hallelujah!

As they marched forth in everything they did as the ministry of Christ in the end times, these people were ministering to the multitudes over the face of the earth. Tens of thousands, even millions seemed to come to the Lord Jesus Christ as these people stood forth and gave the message of the kingdom, of the coming kingdom, in this last hour. It was so glorious, but it seems as though there were those that rebelled, and they would become angry and they tried to attack those workers that were giving the message.

God is going to give to the world a demonstration in this last hour as the world has never known. These men and women are of all walks of life, degrees will mean nothing. I saw these workers as they were going over the face of the earth. When one would stumble and fall, another would come and pick him up. There were no "big I" and "little you" but every mountain was brought low and every valley was exalted, and they seemed to have one thing in common — there was a divine love, a divine love that seemed to flow forth from these people as they worked together, and as they lived together. It was the most glorious sight that I have ever know, Jesus Christ was the theme of their life. They continued and it seemed the days went by as I stood and beheld this sight. I could only cry, and sometimes I laughed. It was so wonderful as these people went throughout the face of the whole earth, bringing forth in this last end time.

As I watched from the very heaven itself, there were times when great deluges of this liquid light seemed to fall upon great congregations, and that congregation would lift their hands and seemingly praise God for hours and even days as the Spirit of God came upon them. God said, "I will pour my Spirit upon all flesh," and that is exactly this thing. And to every man and every woman that received this power, and the anointing of God, the miracles of God, there was no ending to it.

We have talked about miracles. We have talked about signs and wonders, but I could not help but weep as I read again this morning, at 4 o'clock this morning the letter from our native workers. This is only the evidence of the beginning for one man, a "do-nothing, an unheard-of" who would go and stretch forth his hand and say, "In the name of the Lord Jesus Christ, I command life to flow into your body." I dropped to my knees and began to pray again, and I said, "Lord, I know that this thing is coming to pass, and I believe it's coming soon!"

And then again, as these people were going about the face of the earth, a great persecution seemed to come from every angle.

Suddenly there was another great clap of thunder, that seemed to resound around the world, and I heard again the voice, the voice that seemed to speak, "Now this is my people. This is my beloved bride," and when the voice spoke, I looked upon the earth and I could see the lakes and the mountains. The graves were opened and people from all over the world, the saints of all ages, seemed to be rising. And as they rose from the grave, suddenly all these people came from every direction. From the east and the west, from the north and the south, and they seemed to be forming again this gigantic body. As the dead in Christ seemed to be rising first, I could hardly comprehend it. It was so marvelous. It was so far beyond anything I could ever dream or think of.

But as this body suddenly began to form, and take shape again, it took shape again in the form of this mighty giant, but this time it was different. It was arrayed in the most beautiful gorgeous white. Its garments were without spot or wrinkle as its body began to form, and the people of all ages seemed to be gathered into this body, and slowly, slowly, as it began to form up into the very heavens, suddenly from the heavens above, the Lord Jesus came, and became the head, and I heard another clap of thunder that said, "This is my beloved bride for whom I have waited. She will come forth even tried by fire. This is she that I have loved from the beginning of time."

As I watched, my eyes suddenly turned to the far north, and I saw seemingly destruction: men and women in anguish and crying out, and buildings in destruction.

Then I heard again, the fourth voice that said. "Now is My wrath being poured out upon the face of the earth." From the ends of the whole world, the wrath of God seemed to be poured out and it seemed that there were great vials of God's wrath being poured out upon the face of the earth. I can remember it as though it happened a moment ago. I shook and trembled as I beheld the awful sight of seeing the cities, and whole nations going down into destruction.

I could hear the weeping and wailing. I could hear people crying. They seemed to cry as they went into caves, but the caves in the mountains opened up.

They leaped into water, but the water would not drown them. There was nothing that could destroy them. They were wanting to take their lives, but they could not.

Then again I turned my eyes to this glorious sight, this body arrayed in beautiful white, shining garments. Slowly, slowly, it began to lift from the earth, and as it did, I awoke. What a sight I had behld! I had seen the end-time ministries — the last hour. Again on July 27, at 2:30 in the morning, the same revelation, the same vision came again exactly as it did before.

My life has been changed as I realized that we are living in that end time, for all over the world God is anointing men and women with this ministry. It will not be doctrine. It will not be a churchianity. It is going to be Jesus Christ. They will give forth the word of the Lord and are going to say, "I heard it so many times in the vision and according to my word it shall be done."

Oh, my people, listen to me. According to my word, it shall be done. We are going to be clothed with power and anointing from God. We won't have to preach sermons, we won't have to have persons heckle us in public. We won't have to depend on man, nor will we be denomination echoes, but we will have the power of the living God. We will fear no man, but will go in the name of the Lord of Hosts!

Source: https://bit.ly/3hpuE2E

THERE IS HOPE

If you truly understand the things that I have shared with you in this book, and if you truly grasp the fact that they really are going to happen, it can be easy to be filled with dread.

All of our lives are about to change in a major way, and nothing will ever be the same again.

But just because we are entering the most difficult time in all of human history, that doesn't mean that your life is over.

In fact, the greatest chapters of your life can still be ahead of you, but you have got to be willing to surrender your own plans for your life and embrace what God has planned for you.

Yes, things are going to get really, really, really bad, but I want you to know that there is hope.

If you belong to the Lord Jesus Christ, you are under His protection, and He has a plan for you. It may not look anything like what you originally envisioned, and that is okay because His plans are better than our plans anyway.

But if you don't belong to the Lord Jesus Christ, there is no hope. As unprecedented judgments hit our planet, everything that you thought your life would be about is going to be stripped away from you, society is going to fall apart all around you, and there is a very good chance that you will end up dead at some point during the chaotic years to come. Then after you die you will be facing an eternity without God, and that is a fate that is more horrific than you can possibly imagine. So if you have not given your life to Jesus Christ, I would move directly to the next section of this book entitled "The Most Important Thing", because inviting Jesus Christ to be your Lord and Savior is the most important thing that you could possibly do at this moment.

For the rest of you, I want to try to end this book on a very high note. As I discussed in the last chapter, the greatest move of God in the history of the world is coming. Even as our world spins wildly out of control, God is going to be doing things that are absolutely amazing.

But if we choose to be paralyzed by fear, anguish and despair because of all the bad things that are happening, we are totally going to miss out on everything that God has for us in this hour.

There are some people out there that call me a "doom and gloomer" because of all the horrible things that I am warning about. But of course I am just telling the truth. If we had followed God's instructions and lived the way that He wanted us to live, things would have turned out very differently. Instead, we have chosen to be in deep rebellion against God and His ways for decades, and anyone that thought that there would never be any consequences was just being delusional.

Yes, many of the things that I talk about are truly nightmarish. But my wife and I are not down, we are not depressed and we are not defeated. As I mentioned in an earlier chapter, U.S. doctors write more than 250 million prescriptions for antidepressants each year, but they will never write any of those prescriptions for us. In fact, we are not on any medications at all. We are very excited to be living during this time in history, and we believe that the greatest chapters of our lives are still ahead of us.

But do you want to know who is going to be overwhelmed by

fear, despair and depression during the times that are ahead?

The vast majority of the population will be absolutely blind-sided by what is coming. Most people have never even heard about the prophetic warnings in this book, they have no idea what is ahead of us, and once these things start happening they will have no idea why they are taking place. All they will know is that their lives are being destroyed, and the horrific things that they will see all around them will literally drive many of them insane. Many will turn to drugs to dull the pain, others will turn to alcohol, and we will see multitudes of people commit suicide.

Even many believers will feel like they have no hope, because most of them never heard in advance that these things were coming, and most of their churches were completely silent concerning the judgment of America.

Please help me in spreading the message of this book as widely as possible. In particular, get paperback copies and distribute them to everyone that you can. A time will come when this sort of information is not allowed on the Internet, and there will be times when the Internet is not available in some areas at all. But if people have hard copies of this book in their hands, it won't matter if they can't use the Internet to access this information.

There is hope in understanding what is coming, there is hope in getting prepared, and there is hope in surrendering to God's plan.

After reading this book, there will inevitably be people that write me emails asking what I think they should do.

And here is the short answer...

I don't know.

I am not saying that to be glib. The truth is that God's plan is different for each one of us, and the key is to seek to be right in the center of His will for you specifically.

For example, as we approach the fall of America, God is going to call some people to stay and He is going to call some people to go.

In many instances, those that are called to stay in the U.S. will have a much more difficult path, but if that is God's will for you that is what you will need to do. He is more than able to protect you, He is more than able to provide for you, and He is more than able to fulfill the purposes that He has for you.

But that doesn't mean that you are to stay where you are currently. God has been moving people away from both coasts and away from the major cities for many years, and I expect that to continue.

And at some point you may be called to join one of the "cities of light" or "cities of refuge" in the U.S. that some of the prophetic voices have seen pop up during the hard times that are coming.

For those that are called to leave the U.S., you will need to go to whatever country the Lord is directing you.

Many believers will be called to join a great exodus to the land of Israel. Throughout the second half of the Old Testament, we find numerous passages that describe the regathering of all 12 tribes of Israel to the land of Abraham, Isaac and Jacob in the last days. The house of Israel (also known as the house of Ephraim in the Scriptures) will finally be reunited with the house of Judah, and they will never be divided again. This is what Ezekiel 37:15-23 tells us…

15 The word of the Lord came again unto me, saying,

16 Moreover, thou son of man, take thee one stick, and write upon it, For Judah, and for the children of Israel his companions: then take another stick, and write upon it, For Joseph, the stick of Ephraim and for all the house of Israel his companions:

17 And join them one to another into one stick; and they shall become one in thine hand.

18 And when the children of thy people shall speak unto thee, saying, Wilt thou not shew us what thou meanest by these?

19 Say unto them, Thus saith the Lord God; Behold, I will take the stick of Joseph, which is in the hand of Ephraim, and the tribes of Israel his fellows, and will put them with him, even with the stick of Judah, and make them one stick, and they shall be one in mine hand.

20 And the sticks whereon thou writest shall be in thine hand before their eyes.

21 And say unto them, Thus saith the Lord God; Behold, I will take the children of Israel from among the heathen, whither they be gone, and will gather them on every side, and bring them into their own land:

22 And I will make them one nation in the land upon the mountains of Israel; and one king shall be king to them all: and they shall be no more two nations, neither shall they be divided into two kingdoms any more at all.

23 Neither shall they defile themselves any more with their idols, nor with their detestable things, nor with any of their transgressions: but I will save them out of all their dwellingplaces, wherein they have sinned, and will cleanse them: so shall they be my people, and I will be their God.

And Jeremiah 23:7-8 makes it clear that this coming exodus will be so great that it will even make the first exodus pale in comparison…

7 Therefore, behold, the days come, saith the Lord, that they shall no more say, The Lord liveth, which brought up the children of Israel out of the land of Egypt;

8 But, The Lord liveth, which brought up and which led the seed of the house of Israel out of the north country, and from all countries whither I had driven them; and they shall dwell in their own land.

There are numerous prophecies in the Scriptures that warned that the people of the northern 10 tribes (the house of Israel) would be removed from their land and would be scattered among all the nations of the Earth, and those prophecies were precisely fulfilled.

And there are also prophecies that these tribes will eventually be brought back to the exact place they lived before and be fully reunited with the house of Judah. One of the places we find this is at the end of Hosea chapter 1…

10 Yet the number of the children of Israel shall be as the sand of the sea, which cannot be measured nor numbered; and it shall come to pass, that in the place where it was said unto them, Ye are not my people, there it shall be said unto them, Ye are the sons of the living God.

11 Then shall the children of Judah and the children of Israel be gathered together, and appoint themselves one head, and they shall come up out of the land: for great shall be the day of Jezreel.

And in Hosea chapter 3 we are told that the return of the house of Israel will occur "in the latter days"…

5 Afterward shall the children of Israel return, and seek the Lord their God, and David their king; and shall fear the Lord and his goodness in the latter days.

In recent decades, a theory that the 10 tribes of the house of Israel are "lost" and are no longer in God's plans has gained a lot of traction, but that theory is not true at all.

In fact, in Revelation chapter 7 we read that they have a very prominent role in God's plans for the last days, and in Revelation chapter 21 we find that the names of the tribes of Israel are actually written on the gates of New Jerusalem…

12 And had a wall great and high, and had twelve gates, and at the gates twelve angels, and names written thereon, which are the names of the twelve tribes of the children of Israel

There is so much more that could be said about all of this, and in this chapter I have just given you a very, very brief introduction.

The bottom line is that Israel is going to be right at the center of what God is doing in these last days, and God may call you to be part of it.

But ultimately you need to go wherever God is calling you to go, and you need to do whatever it is that He is calling you to do.

His plan for my wife and I may be very different from His plan for you, and there is nothing wrong with that.

We all have a role to play, and we all have a job to do in these last days.

During the months and years to come, a lot of people will be wondering why God would allow these things to happen, and many will feel like God has abandoned them.

But if you know the Lord Jesus Christ, God is not going to abandon you. He will be right there with you through it all, and He placed you at this moment in history for a reason.

So please do not fear the things that are to come. God didn't send us all of these prophetic warnings so that we would be afraid. Rather, he sent them to us so that we wouldn't be afraid.

God knew that all of these things would happen in advance, He is in control, and He has a plan.

Everything that can be shaken will be shaken, and all of this shaking will shake multitudes into the Kingdom.

All of human history has been building up to a great crescendo, and you and I are here to see it. What a tremendous opportunity we have been given, and let us endeavor to do our very best to make the most of it.

Those that have come before us have set the stage for this moment, and now they have passed the baton to us. May we run this race with everything that we have got inside of us, and let us pray that when we finally get home that we will hear these words...

"Well done, good and faithful servant."

As I mentioned all the way back in the first chapter, this is a book of hope. For many of you, I believe that God is going to awaken a fire in your heart as you read this book. He is starting to do something really big, and I believe that He will call many of you to be part of it.

May we all respond to His call, and may we all be strong and courageous during the very dark times that are ahead.

Without God, nothing is possible, but with Him all things are possible.

We shall face the storms ahead with determination, we shall take our stand against all the attacks of the enemy, and in the end we shall be welcomed home to an eternal inheritance that nobody can ever take away from us.

Our God is an awesome God, and we shall serve Him both now and forevermore.

THE MOST IMPORTANT THING

I know that a lot of the information in this book is very troubling. We are heading into the most challenging time in all of human history, and a lot of people are not going to be able to handle the things that are coming.

The good news is that there is hope. If you have made Jesus your Lord and Savior, you have a future ahead of you that is brighter than you can even imagine right now. If you have been reading this book and you have been thinking that you are not sure if you belong to Jesus or not, I very strongly encourage you to read the rest of this chapter very carefully. The good news is that you can know for certain where you will spend eternity, and God wants you to be part of His family.

Yes, the years immediately ahead of us are going to be extremely challenging. And if you are a Christian, you will likely face great persecution for what you believe.

But things are going to be even harder for those that do not know Jesus. Personally, I have no idea how anyone is going to make it through what is coming without a strong relationship with God. I know that I wouldn't want to face the years ahead without Him.

And it is a fact that this life does not go on indefinitely. There are some people that get insurance policies for just about anything and everything, but they don't even give a second thought to what will happen to them once they die.

At the end of every book that I write, I include a chapter that addresses the most important thing that I could possibly talk about. If I had not given my life to the Lord Jesus Christ, I would probably be dead today. He has taken the broken pieces of my life and has turned them into a beautiful thing, and He can do the same thing for you.

If you would like to know how you can become a Christian, I urge you to keep reading. A lot of the time people find Christianity to be very confusing. In the following pages, I have tried to explain the core of the Christian faith in a way that hopefully just about everyone will be able to grasp.

Fortunately, the gospel is very, very easy to understand, and the stakes are incredibly high.

If Christianity is true, then it is possible to have eternal life.

I am not just talking about living for millions of years or billions of years.

I am talking about living for eternity.

If you had the opportunity to live forever, would you take it? Many people would respond to that question by saying that they are not sure if living forever in a world like ours would be desirable, but what if you could live forever in a world where everything had been set right?

What if you could live forever in a perfect world where there is no more evil or suffering or pain?

Would you want that?

The truth is that this is exactly what God wants for you. He loves you very much and He wants to spend forever with you.

If you could, would you want to spend forever with Him?

If God is real, and there really is an afterlife, who wouldn't want to spend eternity with Him?

To be honest with you, if eternal life really exists, there is not a single issue of greater importance for every man, woman and child on the entire planet.

Who would not be willing to give up everything that they own to live forever in paradise surrounded by people that love them?

All over the world people perform all kinds of religious acts, desperately hoping that they will gain favor with God. Some religious nuts even blow themselves up during suicide attacks, hoping that their "sacrifices" will earn them favor with God. But are those really ways to get to heaven?

Of course not.

God did not make it complicated to reach out to Him. The truth is that the plan of salvation described in the Bible is very simple.

It starts with God.

The Bible tells us that God created humanity and that He loves us very much.

In fact, God loves you more than you could possibly ever imagine. The Scriptures go on and on about how great the love of God is and about how deeply He cares for each one of us individually.

But there is a huge problem.

The problem is that humanity is in deep rebellion against God. Humanity has rejected God and is continually breaking His laws.

Most people like to think of themselves as "good" people, but the truth is that none of us is truly "good". Each one of us has broken God's laws over and over again, and we are lawbreakers and criminals in the sight of God.

Perhaps you think that you are a "good person" and that God should let you into heaven based on how good you are.

If that is what you believe, ask yourself this question...

Have you ever broken God's laws?

Posted below is a summary of the Ten Commandments. Are you guilty of violating His ways?...

#1) You shall have no other gods before Me. (There is only one true God – the Creator of all things. Have you ever served a different God? Have you ever dabbled in witchcraft, the occult or other pagan forms of spirituality? Have you ever participated in activities or ceremonies that honor other gods?)

#2) You shall not make any idols. You shall not bow down to them or serve them. (The Scriptures tell us that we are to love God with everything that we have inside of us. Even if you have never bowed down to an idol or a statue, you may have created a "god" in your own mind that you are more comfortable with. That is sin. In fact, we are not to have any "idols" in our lives that we love more than God.)

#3) You shall not take the name of the Lord your God in vain. (Have you ever used God's holy name as a profanity or as a curse word? Have you ever failed to give His holy name the honor that it deserves?)

#4) Remember the Sabbath Day, to keep it holy. (Is there anyone alive that has kept this commandment perfectly?)

#5) Honor your father and mother. (Have you ever been rebellious or disrespectful to your father or your mother even one time? If so, you have broken this commandment.)

#6) You shall not murder. (Even if you have never killed anyone, it is important to remember that Jesus considers hatred to be very similar to murder.)

#7) You shall not commit adultery. (Sexual promiscuity is absolutely rampant in our society today, but you don't even have to sleep with someone to break this commandment. In Matthew 5:27-28, Jesus said that "whosoever looketh on a woman to lust after her hath committed adultery with her already in his heart".)

#8) You shall not steal. (Have you ever stolen anything from someone else? It doesn't matter if it was valuable or not. If you stole something, you are a thief.)

#9) You shall not lie. (Have you ever told a lie? If so, you are guilty of breaking this commandment.)

#10) You shall not covet. (Have you ever jealously desired something that belongs to someone else? This sin is often the first step toward other sins.)

The first four commandments are about loving God. In the

Scriptures, you are commanded to love God with all of your heart, all of your soul, all of your mind and all of your strength.

The final six commandments are about loving others. In the Scriptures, you are commanded to love others as you love yourself.

Have you always loved God and loved others like you should have? *This means everyone even immigrants, refugees etc.*

Sadly, the truth is that we are all guilty of breaking God's laws. In fact, if we took an honest look at how guilty we truly are we would be absolutely horrified.

Take a moment and imagine the following scenario...

One of the biggest television networks has decided to do a huge two hour prime time special all about your life. It is going to be heavily advertised, and tens of millions of people are going to watch it.

Doesn't that sound great?

But instead of a two hour documentary about how wonderful you are, the network has discovered all of the most evil and horrible things that you have ever thought, said or did and they are going to broadcast those things to tens of millions of people all over the world for two hours during prime time.

What would you do if that happened?

Sadly, the truth is that whoever that happened to would be utterly ashamed and would never want to be seen in public again.

Why?

Because we have all done, said and thought things that are unspeakably evil.

We are all sinners in the eyes of God, just as the Scriptures tell us...

"For all have sinned, and come short of the glory of God" (Romans 3:23)

God created us to have fellowship with Him, but He also gave humanity the ability to choose. Unfortunately, humanity has chosen to be in deep rebellion against God and we have all repeatedly broken His laws. When we broke God's commandments, our fellowship with God was also broken. By breaking God's commandments, we decided that our will would be done instead of God's will. And if you look around the world today, you can see the results. Evil and suffering are everywhere. God hates all of this evil and suffering very much. In the Bible, our rebellion against God is called sin.

As a result of our sin, the Scriptures tell us that we are separated from God...

"The wages of sin is death" [spiritual separation from God] (Romans 6:23)

Why doesn't God just forget about our sins?

Well, the truth is that God cannot just sweep our evil under the rug. If God did that, He would cease to be just.

For example, how would you feel about a judge that decided to issue a blanket pardon for Hitler and all of the other high level Nazis for the horrible things that they did?

Would that be a "good" judge?

Of course not.

There is a penalty for evil, and because God is just, that penalty must be paid.

The good news is that Jesus Christ paid the penalty for our sins by dying for us on the cross. He took the punishment that we deserved...

"But God commendeth his love toward us, in that, while we were yet sinners, Christ died for us." (Romans 5:8)

We were guilty, but the Son of God, Jesus Christ, died in our place.

Being fully man, Jesus could die for the sins of mankind.

Being fully God, Jesus could die for an infinite number of sins.

He was mocked, He was beaten, He was scourged ruthlessly and He was nailed to a wooden cross. He was totally innocent, but He was willing to suffer and die because He loved you that much.

Jesus paid the penalty for all of our sins so that fellowship with God could be restored.

Not only that, but Jesus proved that He is the Son of God by rising from the dead...

"Christ died for our sins...He was buried...He rose again the third day according to the Scriptures" (1 Corinthians 15:3-4)

You see, if there was any other way for us to be reconciled to God, Jesus would not have had to die on the cross. He could have just told us to follow one of the other ways to get to heaven. But there was no other way. The death of Jesus on the cross is the only payment for our sins and He is the only way that we are going to get to heaven. In the Scriptures, Jesus put it this way...

"I am the way, the truth, and the life: no man cometh unto the Father, but by me." (John 14:6)

But it is not enough just for you to intellectually know that Jesus is the Son of God and that He died on the cross for our sins.

The Scriptures tell us that we must individually commit our lives to Jesus Christ as Savior and Lord. When we give our lives to Jesus, He forgives our sins and He gives us eternal life...

"But as many as received him, to them gave he power to become the sons of God, even to them that believe on his name" (John 1:12)

"For God so loved the world, that he gave his only begotten Son, that whosoever believeth in him should not perish, but have everlasting life." (John 3:16)

"That if thou shalt confess with thy mouth the Lord Jesus, and shalt believe in thine heart that God hath raised him from the dead, thou shalt be saved." (Romans 10:9)

So exactly how does someone do this?

It is actually very simple.

The Scriptures tell us that it is through faith that we enter into a relationship with Jesus Christ...

"For by grace are ye saved through faith; and that not of your-selves: it is the gift of God: Not of works, lest any man should boast." (Ephesians 2:8,9)

If you are not a Christian yet, then Jesus is standing at the door of your heart and He is knocking. He is hoping that you will let Him come in. He loves you very much and He wants to have a relationship with you...

[Jesus speaking] "Behold, I stand at the door, and knock: if any man hear my voice, and open the door, I will come in to him" (Revelation 3:20)

Jesus asks that you give Him complete control of your life. That means renouncing all of the sin in your life and making Him your Savior and Lord. Just to know intellectually that Jesus died on the cross and that He rose from the dead is not enough to become a Christian. Having a wonderful emotional experience is not enough to become a Christian either. You become a Christian by faith. It is an act of your will.

Are you ready to make a commitment to Jesus Christ?

If you are ready to invite Jesus Christ into your life, it is very easy.

Just tell Him.

God is not really concerned if you say the right words. What He is concerned about is the attitude of your heart.

If you are ready to become a Christian, the following is a prayer that can help you express that desire to Him...

"Lord Jesus, I want to become a Christian. I know that I am a sinner, and I thank you for dying on the cross for my sins. I believe that you are the Son of God and that you rose from the dead. I repent of my sins and I open the door of my life and ask you to be my Savior and Lord. I commit my life to you. Thank you for forgiving all of my sins and giving me eternal life. Take control of my life and make me the kind of person that you want me to be. I will live my life for you. Amen."

If you are ready to enter into a personal relationship with Jesus Christ, then I invite you to pray this prayer right now. Jesus will come into your life, just as He has promised that He would.

If you just invited Jesus Christ to come into your life, you can have 100 percent certainty that you have become a Christian and that you will go to heaven when you die. In 1 John 5:11-13, the Scriptures tell us the following...

"And this is the record, that God hath given to us eternal life, and this life is in his Son. He that hath the Son hath life; and he that hath not the Son of God hath not life. These things have I written unto you that believe on the name of the Son of God; that ye may know that ye have eternal life".

Do you understand what that means?

It means that you can know that you have eternal life.

The Bible says that if you have invited Jesus Christ into your life, your sins are forgiven and you now have eternal life.

What could be better than that?

But your journey is not done.

In fact, it is just beginning.

The Christian life is not easy - especially if you try to go it alone.

There are four keys to spiritual growth for any Christian...

#1) The Bible - If you do not have a Bible you will need to get one and read it every day. It is God's instruction book for your life.

#2) Prayer – Prayer does not have to be complicated. The truth is that prayer is simply talking with God. God wants to hear from you every day, and He will fundamentally transform your life as you pray to Him with humility and sincerity.

#3) Fellowship - The Scriptures tell us that we all need each other. Find a fellowship of local Christians that believe the Bible and that sincerely love one another. They will help you grow.

#4) Witnessing - Tell others about the new life that you have found in Jesus Christ. Helping even one person find eternal life is of more value than anything else that you could ever accomplish in this world.

If you have invited Jesus Christ to come into your life, I would love to hear from you. You can write to me at the following email address...

TheEconomicCollapseBlog @ Hotmail.com

We are entering a period of time that the Bible refers to as the last days. It will be a period of great darkness and the world is going to become increasingly unstable. According to Jesus, there has never been a time like it before, and there will never be a time like it again. But in the middle of all of this, God is going to do great things. He is raising up a Remnant that will keep His commandments, that will boldly proclaim the gospel of salvation through faith in Jesus Christ to the entire world, and that will see their message confirmed by the power of the Holy Spirit just like the very first believers in Jesus did. This is already happening all over the globe even though no organization is in charge of it. And we know for certain that this Remnant will exist in the last days because the Bible tells us that it will (Revelation 12:17; Revelation 14:12). God is starting to bring things full circle. The Remnant of the last days is going to do things the way that the Christians of the first century did things. Have you ever wondered why so many Christian churches today do not resemble what you see in the Bible? Well, the sad truth is that over the centuries churches got away from doing the things that the Scriptures tell us to do, but now God is restoring all things. Without God we can do nothing, but with God all things are possible.

Today, we have an even greater opportunity than the first century Christians did in some ways. During the first century, there were only about 200 million people on this planet. Today, there are more than 7 billion. That means that there are about 35 times as many people living on the planet today than there were back then.

The global population has experienced exponential growth over the past couple of centuries, and that means that we have the opportunity to impact more lives than anyone else ever has. I believe that the greatest move of God that the world has ever seen is coming, and I believe that millions upon millions of souls will be brought into the kingdom during the years ahead. I encourage you to be a part of what is happening.

As the global economy collapses and unprecedented troubles break out around the globe, people are going to be looking for answers. Hundreds of millions of people will have their lives totally turned upside down and will be consumed with despair. Instead of giving in to fear like everyone else will be, it will be a great opportunity for the people of God to rise up and take the message of life to a lost and dying world.

Yes, there will be great persecution. The world system absolutely hates the gospel, and the Bible tells us that eventually Christians will be hunted down and killed for what they believe.

But those that have read the end of the book know that we win in the end. The Bible tells us that Jesus is coming back, and He will reign forever and ever. God loves you very much and He wants to make your life a greater adventure than you ever imagined that it possibly could be. Yes, there will be hardships in this world, but if you are willing to pursue God with a passion and become totally sold out for Him, you can make an eternal difference in countless lives.

When you get a chance, go read the book of Acts. Do you want your own life to look like that?

It can.

In these last days, those that have a passion for God and a passion for reaching the lost are going to turn this world upside down with the gospel of Jesus Christ.

The Scriptures tell us that "there is joy in the presence of the angels of God over one sinner that repents." When even a single person makes a commitment to Jesus Christ, there is great celebration in heaven.

As millions upon millions of precious souls are brought into the kingdom in the years ahead, what do you think the atmosphere in heaven is going to look like?

Yes, darkness and evil will also prosper in the days ahead. A one world government, a one world economy and a one world religion are coming. This world system will utterly hate the Remnant and will try to crush us with everything that they have got.

It is going to take great strength and great courage to stand against the world system in the times that are coming. You have the opportunity to be a part of a greater adventure than anything that Hollywood ever dreamed up, and in the end it may cost you your life.

But in Revelation chapter 2, Jesus promises us that if we are "faithful unto death" that He will give us "a crown of life".

For those of us that have a relationship with Jesus, we know that we have an eternity with God ahead of us. Jesus has forgiven our sins and has given us eternal life, and nobody can ever take that away from us.

Life is like a coin – you can spend it any way that you want, but you can only spend it once.

Spend your life on something that really matters.

God is raising up a Remnant that is going to shake the world, and you do not want to miss out on the great move of God that is coming. It is going to be unlike anything that any of us have ever seen before.

If you enjoyed this book, I encourage you to also connect with me on the Internet. You can find my work at the following websites...

The Economic Collapse Blog: http://theeconomiccollapseblog.com/

End Of The American Dream: http://endoftheamerican-dream.com/

The Most Important News: http://themostimportant-news.com/

Thank you for taking the time to read this book to the end. I would love to hear any feedback that you may have. Just like the rest of you, I am always learning.

My wife and I are praying for you, and for all of those that will end up reading this book.

May the Lord bless you and keep you.

May the Lord make His face shine upon you and be gracious to you.

May the Lord lift up His countenance upon you and give you His peace.

Amen.

ABOUT THE AUTHOR

Michael Snyder

Michael is a voice crying out for change in a society that generally seems content to stay asleep. For the past decade, Michael has consistently been one of the most popular authors on the Internet. Collectively, his articles on The Economic Collapse Blog, End Of The American Dream and The Most Important News have been viewed more than 100 million times. His articles are also republished on dozens of other prominent websites all over the globe where they are read countless more times. Michael has written four other books that are available on Amazon.com including The Beginning Of The End, The Rapture Verdict, and Living A Life That Really Matters. By purchasing those books you help to support his work. During these very challenging times, people need hope more than ever before, and it is Michael's goal to share the gospel of Jesus Christ with as many people as he possibly can.

CPSIA information can be obtained
at www.ICGtesting.com
Printed in the USA
LVHW021959240722
724285LV00008B/480